DOUGHERTY

INTERSECTIONS
ARCHITECTURE AND
SOCIAL RESPONSIBILITY

DOUGHERTY

ARCHITECTS LLP

To the teachers at the College of Environmental Design at the University of California Berkeley
who, in the late 1960s, challenged us to see beyond individual buildings
to emphasize their impact on the community.

To our clients, who have entrusted us to give form to their dreams and aspirations.

To our families, who have supported us with their love and devotion.

To the Earth, from which we have borrowed resources to create the places we design.

DOUGHERTY + DOUGHERTY

ARCHITECTS LLP

INTERSECTIONS
ARCHITECTURE AND
SOCIAL RESPONSIBILITY

images
Publishing

Published in Australia in 2008 by

The Images Publishing Group Pty Ltd

ABN 89 059 734 431

6 Bastow Place, Mulgrave, Victoria 3170, Australia

Tel: +61 3 9561 5544 Fax: +61 3 9561 4860

books@imagespublishing.com

www.imagespublishing.com

Copyright © The Images Publishing Group Pty Ltd 2008

The Images Publishing Group Reference Number: 778

National Library of Australia Cataloguing-in-Publication entry:

Title:	Dougherty + dougherty : intersections: architecture and social responsibility.
ISBN:	978 1 86470 303 0 (hbk.)
Subjects:	Dougherty + Dougherty Architects (Firm)
	Architectural firms—United States.
	Sustainable buildings—Design and construction.
	Architecture—United States—21st century.
Dewey Number:	720.973

Edited by Beth Browne

Designed by The Graphic Image Studio Pty Ltd, Mulgrave, Australia
www.tgis.com.au

Pre-publishing services by Splitting Image Colour Studio Pty Ltd, Australia

Printed by Wai Man Book Binding (China) Ltd.

IMAGES has included on its website a page for special notices in relation to this and our other publications.
Please visit www.imagespublishing.com.

Contents

Foreword

Dougherty + Dougherty
Intersections: Architecture and Social Responsibility

Marvin J. Malecha, FAIA
Dean, North Carolina State University College of Design
2008 AIA First Vice President / 2009 AIA President
ACSA Distinguished Professor, AIA/ACSA Topaz Laureate

The act of building is an ancient necessity instigated by the most primitive needs: shelter, safety, and the facilitation of human life. In its aggregate, the act of building constitutes place, a community revealing the most important values of a society, the stage for the ceremonies of culture as well as the translator of the relative importance of its citizens. When the sophistication of the means of building shelter forms the language of a place as much as the spoken and written word, it can be observed that an architectural culture has evolved. In ancient Greece the Golden Age of Pericles was an intense and amazingly short period of public building, which included some of the most significant temples of all human history that resulted from a long evolutionary process. It was a process begun by addressing the most rudimentary principles of response to a site including topography, wind patterns, and the movement of the sun. It also included a commitment to exceptional building materials, thus transforming primitive construction methods derived from lessons in wood into the stone buildings that resulted. From this period a classical language was derived that is in use today in many true and derivative forms.

To reflect on the work of individuals engaged in the creative process within an architectural practice is to consider the evolution of a language that has evolved through the lessons of application as well as the opportunities presented by the commissions being considered. It is an opportunity to look deeper into any one of the projects presented but it is also possible to consider the single building in the context of a lifetime of work. It is a study of the one among the many and the many given meaning by the one. It is a reflection made more interesting by the partnership of the two people who lead this practice and the collaborative spirit that defines their interaction with those who work alongside them.

The heading of this reflective exercise, *Intersections: Architecture and Social Responsibility*, leaves no doubt about the intentions and aspirations of a lifetime of practice. Each of the chapter titles—Regeneration and

Institution, Community and the Urban Fabric, Culture and Suburbia, Youth and Heritage, and Permanence and Transition—is a subheading of a manifesto born of the Berkeley experience at the very beginning of the architectural education of Brian Dougherty and Betsey Olenick Dougherty and realized through the continuing commitment to the best examples of citizen architecture. The work reflected in this monograph is spirited and thoughtful. It draws its energy from what is expected in the project program in the best interests of the users needs. It is work that possesses considerable personality but it is not necessarily the reflection of the architects' personalities over those who will live and work in the building.

The John T. Lyle Center for Regenerative Studies at California State Polytechnic University, Pomona provides the opportunity for a window into the process that guides the architectural outcomes illustrated in each of the chapters. A university client group led by Professor Lyle had a clear vision of what was needed. Betsey and Brian Dougherty were brought to the project to realize the dream in built form. Even though students and faculty had spent years considering the design for this new center, there was much to be done. The concept of a built community founded on green principles needed to be brought to a form that could be realized meeting conventional building codes and standards. New materials required in-depth review to determine their suitability for a green project. Water systems were considered to make the highest and best use of gray water as well as water purification options. The proximity to an urban landfill required a careful study of gas migration and all manner of related testing instrumentation.

Throughout this period in the project's history, the Dougherty + Dougherty commitment to sustainability never wavered in spite of what seemed to be a painfully slow decision-making process. It was clear that the architectural team had embraced this period as the time of research and development. It was a time when the architectural team conducted a patient search to engage the knowledge and leadership of a faculty and student team passionately leading the University toward sustainable practices—two decades before it was fashionable. The persistence demonstrated in pursuit of the very best answer to the design of the Center for Regenerative Studies and the commitment to address societal imperatives through the work is the story of this publication. It is the subtext. This is the spirit and soul of an architectural practice applying a commitment to client service and the development of new knowledge while remembering the societal imperatives that are inherent in architectural projects.

It is for this reason that I commend this publication as a primer for architects who wish to seek a deeper meaning in their work. It is an exemplar for how the architect may enhance the lives of those who live in their buildings. The range of public work cited in the body of this work belies the expression "good enough for government work." In the hands of Dougherty + Dougherty, good enough for public work is obviously measured by only the highest ideals. How satisfying it is to consider the work of architects who began their careers with the highest of ambitions for the reflection of social responsibility in their work to see it realized without the cynicism of those who seem embattled by their own desire for personal expression. This work is filled with optimism. It is a built expression of the possibility to connect social, and therefore environmental, responsibility with the paths of two ambitious architects. It is an intersection that is explored in this monograph. Like all intersections, careful choreography is sometimes required to come through unscathed. Yet, here is a journey of considerable merit. It is a journey for all of us to ponder.

Regeneration and Institution

We live as organisms within a complex fabric. While our individual actions account for our relationship with that fabric, societal institutions influence how we behave and affect outcomes on a broad scale. Creating architecture at the intersection of these two forces provides us with a compelling opportunity to behave in a way that will impact generations far beyond our own. How can we best transform resources to offer the possibility that, in their altered state, they will give more back to the environment than they have consumed? How can these places transform those who inhabit them from self-focus to a real place in the protection of our future well-being? We carefully select the places we inhabit, touch lightly on the land and intrude as little as possible in the patterns that nature has already established. We build with materials that will have lasting durability and can be most easily replenished. We establish institutions that dwell within structures that invest in the natural surroundings rather than draw from them. We connect those who come to these places with the very nature that gave rise to them and the institutions they have formed.

At our core we need institutions that organize our actions and everyday activities and that give us a foundation from which to reach further as individuals with a common purpose. The effect that the structures designed to house these societal organizations can have on those who both create and inhabit them is profound. Their reach to those outside is both long and long-term. This is our moment to act. To search for the answers to how we will become stewards of the fabric borrowed from our children. While we have yet to find the ideal outcome, the search offers the opportunity to lead us as individuals and the institutions we have created toward a future that will be regenerative. As we learned backpacking in the wilderness as youths, "leave behind only footprints." Our goal is to take that to a higher level and remove even the imprints of our boots.

John Lyle Center for Regenerative Studies

Design/Completion 1990/1997

Pomona, California

California State Polytechnic University Pomona

15,000 square feet

Building structure
Lightweight steel structure and wood framed walls, wood-framed roof structure, conventional concrete spread footings, and raised concrete piers with concrete masonry retaining structures

Building materials
Exterior factory-stained cedar siding, exposed concrete floors, high-performance glazing, standing seam copper roof, paving of recycled concrete and decomposed granite

Truly a watershed project, the genesis for the design began in 1987 with an experimental studio titled the "LandLab Project" with Professor John T. Lyle at the Cal Poly Pomona College of Environmental Design. Conceived in response to a perceived lack of participation on the part of the university to the issues of environmental conservation, the project was envisioned to be an interdisciplinary living, working, research, and classroom village focused on regenerative technologies; providing resources back to the environment in excess of those consumed. The key philosophical principal for all aspects of the project and research is the idea that whatever is developed at this facility is distinctly low-tech, ensuring that these concepts can then be exported to developing countries and utilized to provide a grassroots commitment to resource conservation.

Located in a small valley dotted with walnut trees about 40 miles south of Los Angeles, it is wedged between the university campus and the adjacent regional landfill on a site that can be 120 degrees in the summer and near freezing in the winter. The center is targeted to eventually go "off grid." Solar buildings, reclaimed water systems, aquaculture, and environmental agriculture programs provide a framework for research and experimentation. Phase I provides approximately 14,000 square feet of faculty and student resident housing for 20, kitchen and dining commons, work rooms, lecture and seminar rooms, and administrative offices. Phase II expands academic, faculty and agriculture facilities.

Pre-dating LEED and other formal benchmark programs, much of the original discussion centered on creating a framework of criteria for regenerative construction. These concepts were placed under four broad umbrellas: water, energy, land, and materials. The land was considered first and the site was selected with the goal of minimizing impact to the environment. Nestled into a grove of 70 year old black walnut trees, no trees were cut or disturbed during construction and reshaping of the land was minimized to preserve the

1　A mature center is enhanced by student work and research projects
2　Aquaculture ponds host plants and fish, while providing stormwater collection and site irrigation

1

3 North elevation
4 An overview of the newly opened center illustrates the site development plan
5 The office addition is located at the top of the hill
6 All ceilings provide operable clerestories, fans, and energy efficient lighting

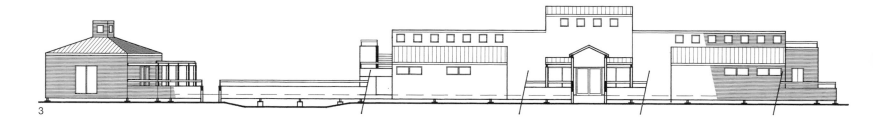

3

4

6

natural drainage and ecosystems. Aquaculture ponds were established to both treat on-site waste and provide a laboratory for plant and animal life. Despite the extreme temperatures, no airconditioning is utilized in the facility. Instead, buildings are partially earth buried or raised above the aquaculture ponds to allow the cooling breezes to cross the water and then condition the spaces. Natural light fills each room through a variety of windows and light shelves. Low-velocity ceiling fans move the air within the spaces to create a level of comfort that otherwise might depend on mechanical conditioning. All materials growing on the site serve multiple purposes. Vines on trellises provide shade, food, and beauty. Plant varieties are selected to re-establish native habitat, provide food, and buffer the inhabitants from the climate.

The greatest challenge in the late 1980s, as the facility was being designed, was finding manufacturers of materials and products that fit the tough criteria for inclusion established by the team. Dougherty + Dougherty vetted products ruthlessly to "bully and coax" the suppliers into thinking green. The real reward in the end was to see a California Green Heron, not seen in this area for decades, gently land at the aquaculture pond to feed on the freshwater tilapia under the shadow of the buildings.

Santa Monica is a community rooted in activism. It is a natural outgrowth of this culture that an awareness and commitment to green design be embedded in the goals for the Ocean Park School. Located in an environmentally sensitive neighborhood, this project grew from a consensus-building series of community workshops. The site is adjacent to a neighborhood park, providing open space for this eclectic environment. Surrounded by residential bungalows and towering palms, the school is a reflection of its independent and creative setting. Each decision shaping the facility has involved the neighborhood, district, teachers, and students at all levels. An interactive process has involved ongoing community workshops, focus sessions, and weekend design forums, all targeted at providing a direct conduit from the people to the design team.

The program brings together two distinct schools on one site. The Santa Monica Alternative School House (SMASH), based upon the Summerhill model of self-directed curriculum, is a magnet for independent learning in the arts. The John Muir School is more traditional and houses a larger student population. Joint-use facilities include an arts and crafts venue, a performing arts/community meeting hall to seat 350, a child-care center, a healthcare clinic, and intramural sports facilities.

Regenerative design is reflected in all elements of the project. The site is a previously developed school site that had been underutilized since a 1933 earthquake damaged the original school structures. An urban garden is included in a prominent location to bring together students and community members to learn the values of biodynamic plants. On-site recycling and composting is integrated into the facility. The site density is increased with primarily two-story structures. Natural light fills each space and views are afforded to all of the surrounding community. Heritage trees have been selected to landscape the site providing both native plantings and history lessons for the children.

Ocean Park
Elementary School

Design/Completion 1992/1997

Santa Monica, California

Santa Monica – Malibu Unified School District

44,000 square feet

Building structure
Steel frame with wood framed walls and roof; conventional concrete foundations with slab on grade

Building materials
Painted exterior plaster with composition roof shingles, high-performance glazing with punched metal sunshades; retractable fabric deck awnings, water conserving fixtures, energy-efficient mechanical and electrical systems

1

1   The front gate at Ocean Park School is an extension of a sculptural fence reflecting
     the waves of the nearby ocean
2   The two-story classroom buildings enable a comprehensive program to be
     accommodated on a small site, orienting to the adjacent joint-use park playfields

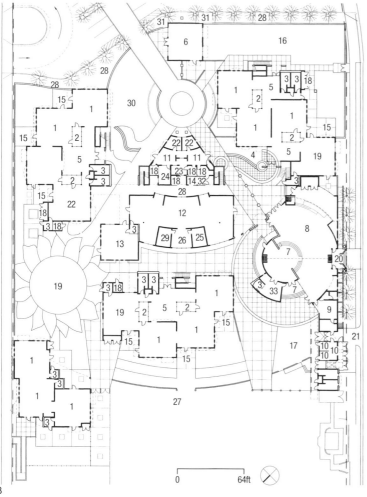

1 Classroom
2 Teacher preparation
3 Toilet
4 Outdoor teaching
5 Shared teaching/technology
6 Arts
7 Stage/performance
8 Multipurpose/performance
9 Food service
10 Site service
11 Administration
12 Media center
13 Community room
14 Elevator
15 Teaching patio
16 Adventure play
17 Lunch area
18 Storage
19 Kindergarten
20 Community access
21 Service access
22 Principal
23 Nurse
24 Conference
25 Book storage
26 Work area
27 Play yard access
28 Sculptured sound wall
29 Equipment storage
30 Environmental study areas
31 School sign
32 Elevator equipment
33 Dressing room

3

4

5

6

3 Site plan
4 Each individual campus-within-a-campus has its own signature buildings
5 The Muir School entrance greets visitors to the campus-within-a-campus
6 The joint-use multipurpose room is host to school and community events and fine arts performances
7 Shared computer labs anchor the first floor of each classroom building
8 Classrooms benefit from a variety of sustainable strategies, including skylighting and shaded natural light, operable windows and ceiling fans, energy-efficient lighting, and tackable acoustical wall panels

7

8

Paving materials incorporate a high level of pervious content reducing stormwater runoff and softening the ground plane. Existing site trees have been protected in place and the buildings are designed to feature these landmarks of the neighborhood. Ocean breezes are captured and utilized to bring thermal comfort to all spaces with the assistance of ceiling fans. Recycled content in materials throughout the project and low-VOC content provides indoor air quality that will ensure the long-term health of the students and staff. Along with on-site rainwater collection numerous other environmental lessons are embedded in elements throughout the project.

The Fullerton Arboretum engages the visitor in education, meditation, recreation, and simple aesthetic delight. The challenge of meeting these needs has presented the arboretum with the opportunity to enhance its physical setting, and set an example of building in harmony with nature.

This is the first of a two-phase project. Housed within 9500 square feet are three classrooms, a catering kitchen, museum space for exhibiting historical agricultural artifacts, and a conference room. The featured area is a large open-air pavilion integrated with a naturally landscaped courtyard and amphitheater. Designed as a sustainable demonstration project, features of the design are focused in a number of key areas.

The arboretum is designed as a sustainable site that touches softly on the land. A series of decisions include: selection of a previously developed site to preserve natural open space, location of the facility near a public bus line, the restoration of previously developed land and a ratio of building to open space that improves on the prior land use, and the use of pervious paving materials including decomposed granite walkways and pervious concrete parking areas. This approach also supports stormwater treatment prior to runoff leaving the site, heat island reduction through the use of light-colored pervious surfaces, and light pollution reduction with directed photometrics.

A number of water-efficient features include the use of water-efficient landscape irrigation and native plant species. Waterless urinals, low-volume toilets, and low-flow faucets yield as much as a 41 percent reduction in water consumption

Creating an energy-efficient building envelope will yield long-term savings in cost and impact to the environment. High-efficiency HVAC units with no CFCs (Puron is used) are utilized. The building exceeds the basic requirements of California Title 24 for energy efficiency and the arboretum is also investigating the opportunity to purchase green power. A selection of

Fullerton Arboretum Visitor Center and Events Pavilion

Design/Completion 2003/2006

Fullerton, California

Fullerton Arboretum/California State University, Fullerton

14,250 square feet
(Masterplanned two phases;
9500 square feet first phase)

Building structure
Wood frame and lightweight steel

Building materials
Factory-finished wood/cement fiber-board siding, standing seam metal roof, exposed concrete slab floors, high-performance glazing, pervious concrete and decomposed granite exterior paving

1

1   The arboretum events pavilion, classrooms, and history museum
2   Outdoor events pavilion

1	Museum	8	Men's restroom	15	Maintenance
2	Pavilion	9	Women's restroom	16	Administration
3	Classroom	10	Interpretive center	17	Service yard
4	Kitchen	11	Gift shop	18	Museum expansion
5	Storage	12	Plaza	19	Parking
6	Meeting room	13	Amphitheatre	20	Bus parking
7	Office	14	Water feature	21	Vehicular drop-off

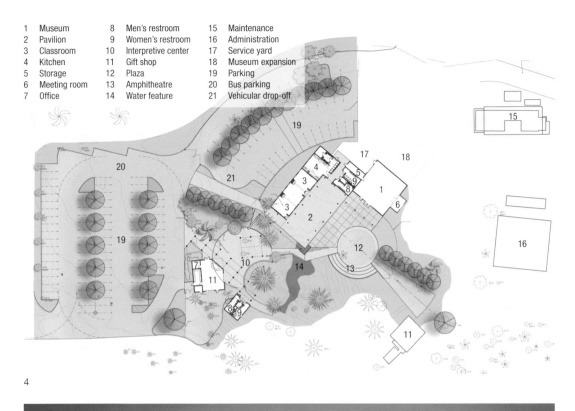

4

direct/indirect energy-efficient lighting fixtures provides a non-glare interior environment, and light controls provide the ability to respond to daylight conditions. Integrated energy-management systems allow local and remote control of HVAC and other systems in the facility.

Materials were collected, sorted, and stored during construction for recycling. Recycled content is specified for steel, drywall, insulation, and flooring. Wood cement board is used for building siding for increased waste material content as well as improved long-term maintenance. Local materials are specified for inclusion in the project in a variety of areas.

5

6

3 The arboretum history museum with hands-on learning opportunities
4 Composite site plan
5 The arboretum museum, reflecting an agrarian history
6 The arboretum pavilion entrance

Apple Valley Town Hall Expansion

Design/Estimated completion
2008/2010

Apple Valley, California

Town of Apple Valley

25,000 square feet

Building structure
Rammed earth on concrete stem walls, engineered wood trusses, structural steel, light-gauge steel

Building materials
Portland cement plaster, metal siding, clay tile, built-up roof, high-performance glazing

The proposed town hall expansion builds upon Dougherty + Dougherty's sustainable approach, tackling another extreme climate, this time at a civic scale. The extreme, dry climate in Apple Valley sees temperature highs above 100 degrees Fahrenheit in the summer and lows below freezing in the winter. The extreme winds prevent the use of operable windows and natural ventilation. The goal is to build a durable building that is integrated with the landscape, low impact, and a comfortable place to both visit and work.

The form of the building echoes elements of both the built and natural context. The color palette is pulled from the surrounding reds and browns present in the site. Massive walls and a swooping clay-tile roof reflect elements of the existing buildings in the complex while also tying in with the contrast of heaviness and lightness inherent in the desert landscape. The entry, created by a rift in the rammed-earth walls, connects the visitor with the earth. Users are protected from the harsh exterior, but remain connected to the surroundings through extensive views, daylighting, and indigenous planting.

The plan brings in users through one of three gathering nodes. These nodes provide places for people to congregate informally and they help to mitigate the transition from the harsh exterior to the more temperate interior. The public community room and conference rooms flank the main paths of travel, with the staff core anchoring the volume of the split-gabled roof. Circulation flows freely through the staff area. Each department runs vertically through the space, leading to the more private spaces at the north.

The support of our forward-thinking client helped to create a sustainable building in this extreme environment. The rammed-earth walls on the south side provide a great deal of thermal mass that helps to mitigate the extreme diurnal temperature swings. Overhangs and trellises provide seasonal shading, keeping direct sunlight out during the summer months and letting it in during the winter months. Daylighting

1

1 A north-facing events patio is protected from the sun and wind
2 The front entry reflects the design elements of the existing civic center
3 The "node" provides a path of travel between buildings, and a gathering place for community events

2

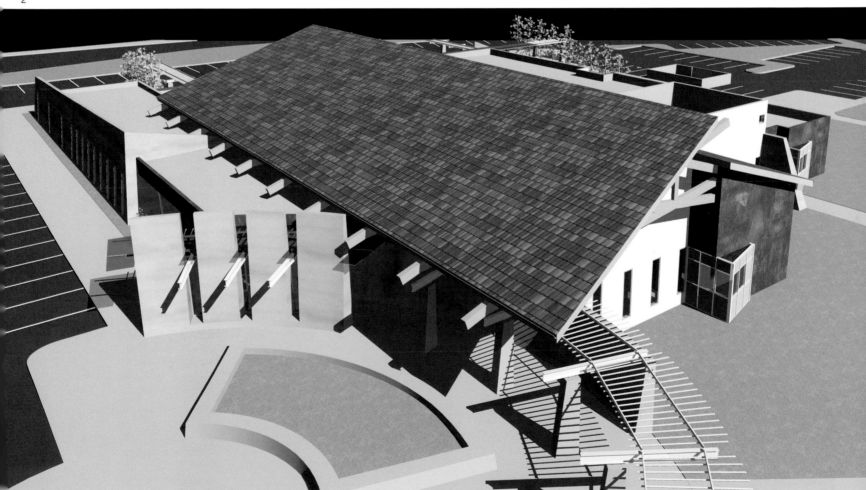

3

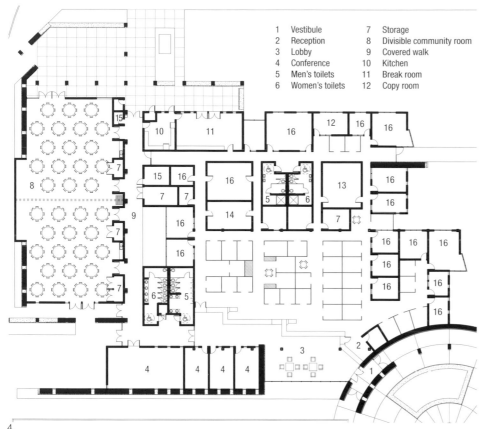

1	Vestibule	7	Storage	13	File room
2	Reception	8	Divisible community room	14	Plan room
3	Lobby	9	Covered walk	15	Electrical
4	Conference	10	Kitchen	16	Offices
5	Men's toilets	11	Break room		
6	Women's toilets	12	Copy room		

4

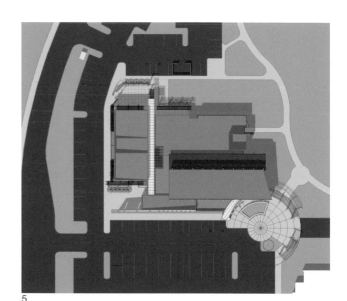

5

6

strategies bring in balanced direct and indirect natural light through clerestories, light shelves, and skylights. Interior daylight sensors automatically dim electric lighting based on natural light levels. A raised floor in the main volume provides under-floor air distribution allowing for efficient heating and cooling, personal climate control, and future organizational flexibility. Sustainable materials are pervasive in the project. Rammed-earth walls use aggregate pulled directly from site excavation and only a small amount of Portland cement. Sustainable finishes include recycled floor tile, recycled carpet, rapidly renewable casework materials, low-VOC adhesives, and formaldehyde-free wood products. Drought tolerant, indigenous landscaping used throughout the current complex is continued with the new project.

Through the contextual form, clear program organization, and sustainable building strategies, the Apple Valley Town Hall expansion provides an environmentally sensitive community hub that will stand as an example of the town's ideals for years to come.

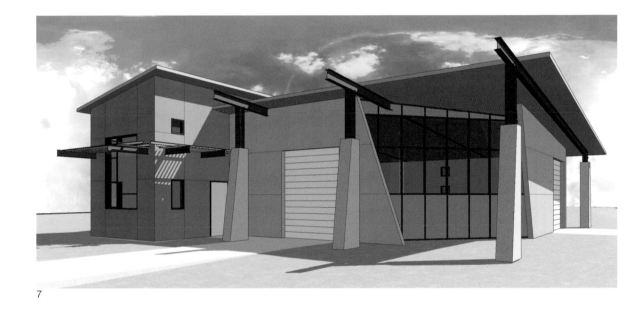

7

4   Floor plan
5   The new town hall building addition completes the civic center and adds a "node" linking the new facility to the existing town hall
6   A secondary entrance serves the town offices and community center
7   A small park-maintenance building provides a shop, storage, and vehicle recharging facilities to service the civic center park

Heller Residence

Design/Completion 1979/1981

Newport Beach, California

Private residence

2900 square feet

Building structure
Wood framed structure with steel moment resisting frames

Building materials
Painted exterior plaster, high-performance glazing, concrete masonry, paver tile floors on the ground level, sliding translucent screened doors

Conceived shortly after the energy crisis of the 1970s, the Heller Residence is the rootstock from which all subsequent Dougherty + Dougherty projects have grown. Located on an island in Newport Harbor with small lots and an informal lifestyle, the challenge was how to maximize the site utilization, minimize energy consumption, and provide a variety of environments for the owners to find both privacy and connection with the outdoors. Rather than creating a structure that would be placed on the site, the design grew from a detailed study of the three-dimensional planning limitations that were governed by the community and how to craft this volume into a matrix of indoor and outdoor rooms connected and separated by light, views, and passages.

Strategies to minimize energy consumption were explored by placing a large greenhouse section to the south with plants and a thickened thermal-mass floor placed just inside. Opening this area to a two-story interior atrium allows the air to flow freely up and out through the operable windows at the top of the atrium. Low windows provide air movement over the thermal mass of the floor and keep the interior temperature even year-round. State-of-the-art equipment was used in the kitchen and throughout the home to minimize energy consumption at all levels. The roof area houses a series of solar hot-water collectors to assist with the provision of domestic hot water. Low-volume irrigation is provided to both the interior and exterior planters to allow for a low-maintenance environment constantly charged with fresh oxygen from the plant life.

The spaces within the home are woven into a tapestry of views and connections. From the deck near the master bedroom one can look over the adjacent properties and connect with the nearby beach. From the adjacent interior balcony one can look out on a rainy day and feel protected by the embrace of the surrounding rooms. As you rise from the two-story living room the eye is drawn from the interior to the exterior to the interior again. Sunlight fills each space, but can be screened for privacy and mood. The ground floor flows from atrium to courtyard and back again.

1   Contextually, the home occupies a narrow lot in a high-density Southern California beach community
2   A simple street façade includes a promontory balcony for views of the nearby harbor

1

3

3 An interior atrium ties indoor and outdoor spaces together while defining an entry between the living room and dining room
4 A second-floor circulation bridge flies over the living room
5 The south-facing greenhouse wall provides a column of ventilation in the summer and solar heat gain in the winter
6 The greenhouse wall glows at night, revealing the indoor–outdoor relationship, visually expanding the narrow lot
7 An outdoor patio on the south side provides a place for enjoying the California sun
8 Second floor plan
9 Site plan

4

5

6

7

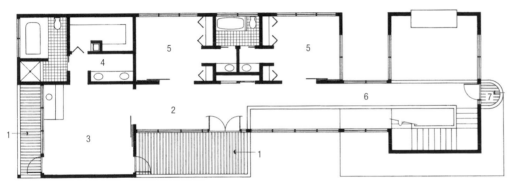

8

1   Deck
2   Solarium
3   Master bedroom
4   Master bathroom
5   Bedroom
6   Bridge
7   Crow's nest

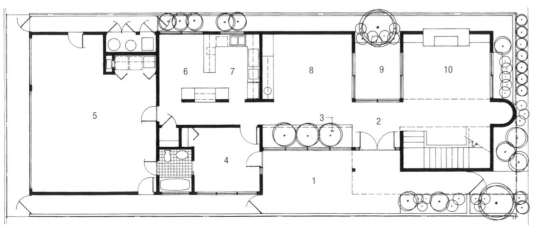

9

1   Entry patio
2   Entry
3   Planter
4   Den/guest room
5   Garage
6   Dining
7   Kitchen
8   Dining room
9   Atrium
10   Living room

0   12ft

Mountain Residence

Design/Completion 2001/2003

Mammoth Lakes, California

Private residence

4600 square feet

Building structure
Wood frame with light steel on a concrete foundation

Building materials
Sustainably harvested lumber, post-consumer recycled decking, interior wood flooring from recycled Thai railroad ties, local stone, cool metal roof, carpet from recycled fibers, ceramic tile from recycled glass, low-VOC paints, low-E insulated glazing, EPA-rated wood-burning fireplace, low-consumption water fixtures, CFL lighting fixtures

The creation of a structure that is tuned to the land is central to this sustainably designed home. Mammoth Lakes is located at an elevation of 8000 feet in the eastern Sierra Mountains. Temperate during the summer and snowbound for much of the winter, Mammoth is a landscape of immense beauty and harsh climate. Heavily forested with large firs and pines, the arid ground plane is sparsely populated with manzanita and indigenous scrub. The location and conceptual elements of the home revealed themselves slowly over a full cycle of the seasons. A small natural clearing allowed for construction with the removal of only five trees from the site. These trees were crafted into furniture for the family. The wind and temperature shaped the building form: tall and sheltering, the interior volume was maximized while the exterior skin was minimized. Snow is scoured away from the entry by the prevailing west wind. Views to the southern and western mountain ranges are framed from each room.

The plan is derived from a simple cruciform around a central core. As a metaphor for the seismic and volcanic heritage of the land, the second floor was rotated on the central axis with a "fault" separating the west and east portions of the space. The resulting interplay between plan and section both connects and separates each activity area. In a home intended to bring together family and friends throughout the year, it is important to provide a nurturing and gathering environment as well as privacy.

A commitment to sitting lightly on the land guided the design of each element of the house. Lumber was selected from a sustainably harvested forest. The flooring for the main level was crafted from reclaimed railroad ties from Thailand. Abandoned on the floor of the rain forest, these century-old timbers from rosewood, teak, mahogany, and other tropical hardwoods sat fallow following the abandonment of the railroad. They were then milled by local artisans and made available for a new use. The house is flooded with natural light filtered through the fir and pine forest and tempered through low-E double glazed windows.

1 The south face lets in light filtered through a natural wooded setting
2 The house is set back into the woods

1

1	Master bedroom	4	Bedroom	7	Deck
2	Master bathroom	5	Bathroom	8	Open to below
3	Studio	6	Stair	9	Elevator

3 The first (below) and second (above) floor plans illustrate the cruciform plan and rotated "leg"
4 Organizational plan
5 The fireplace and stair are centrally located at the core of the cruciform plan
6 The entry is open to three upper levels
7 The master bedroom shares one leg of the cruciform plan
8 The kitchen and dining area are open for casual entertaining; floors on the main level are recycled railroad ties

■ Outdoor/transition space
■ Common area
□ Bedroom
□ Bathroom

Loft

Second floor

First floor

Entry

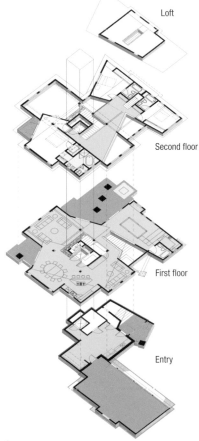

0   12ft

1	Games room	6	Stair
2	Living room	7	Deck
3	Entertainment room	8	Pantry
4	Dining room	9	Elevator
5	Entry	10	Jacuzzi

3

4

5

6

7

The entire site maintains the native planting and utilizes no irrigation. Water consumption is also minimized through the use of low-flow fixtures. All of the lighting in the house is lamped with CFLs. The walls and roof are heavily insulated creating an envelope that remains warm in the winter and cool in the summer with minimal energy consumption. The philosophy of creating a nurturing shelter, which cradles the family within the mantle of the forest while minimizing the carbon footprint, will resonate far into the future.

8

Community and the Urban Fabric

The roar of passing traffic, the jostling crowd, heat and tension—all within a grid of concrete and steel with only the occasional tree—this is our urban fabric. Somehow within this cauldron of energy we look to each other and feel the need for community. Community connects us to each other, to the spiritual elements that balance our lives, and to the need for stability and warmth. We have the ability to create environments that reach out to bring community members together to reflect their common goals and aspirations. These places can lift our spirits and shine a light in the dark. They give us a sheltering roof under which we can play, share, learn, and discuss a future vision or simply gather to celebrate our joint accomplishments. How best to do this? How do we transform the alienating steel and concrete of the urban fabric into the very substance that will bring us together?

A roof reaches out to offer protection from the elements. Windows let us peer in from the surrounding darkness. Windows let us look out at the sunlight and trees. Rooms can be large enough to bring us all together and small enough to nurture an intimate discussion. We build to reflect the common values that unite us as community. We build to provide a space in which our dreams will be recorded for our children to share. In community we find the ability to lift each other toward a future that enriches the experience that unites us. The key is to look for the intersections within the urban fabric rather than the avenues that divide. Timeless materials that belong to the place are more than a physical manifestation of location. Community stands as if on two threads suspended in midair—we hold hands to maintain balance, looking simultaneously toward the sun and the vast canyon below.

Cameron Park Community Center and Gymnasium

Design/Completion 2002/2004

West Covina, California

City of West Covina

24,000 square feet

Building structure
Concrete masonry bearing walls with lightweight steel-framed roof

Building materials
Exposed concrete masonry exterior walls, exposed steel roof structure, metal roof, high-performance glazing, wood flooring in gym and conference room, decorative paver tiles in lobby and entry, recycled fiber content carpet in the game room and offices

This community center is located in a neighborhood park in West Covina. The previous facility had deteriorated and was unable to support community programs. The new design grew from a public workshop process and is home to a wide variety of recreational programs.

The 24,000-square-foot project provides an entry lobby, administrative space and lounge; a youth playroom and pre-function space; a divisible conference/meeting facility and adjacent events patio; a catering kitchen also serving as a lobby concession counter; a double gymnasium, divisible into two full-size basketball or volleyball courts; and toilet rooms with separate locker areas. The building is designed for flexibility, with movable walls between the conference/ meeting rooms and also bisecting the gymnasium. Each function can be locked separately for different operating hours between 6 am and 10 pm, while maintaining access to the kitchen and toilet rooms in a safe and secure manner.

The new community center represents a keystone project in the funding of new community service facilities within the city. The project design is responsive to a public input process that has included community design workshops, committee meetings, planning meetings, and City Council meetings. During programming and design, extensive debate ensued regarding the proportion of conference and meeting space to the gymnasium floor. Neighbors debated the proposed scale of the project and potential traffic, but favored the development of a new building able to support youth athletic programs in place of the dilapidated existing structure. After more than 24 plan concepts, an acceptable approach was approved. The design concept articulates the project elements to minimize the building scale to the street, to create a park-oriented entrance and outdoor gathering area, to preserve the existing mature trees and canopy, and to enhance existing walkways/parkways and parking areas with decorative paving, new planting, and dramatic nighttime lighting.

1

1 The front entry bridges the gymnasium and activity spaces
2 Twilight at the Cameron Park Community Center

4

The Cameron Park Community Center is an overwhelmingly popular destination that opened with the support of a local radio station, an auto show, food vendor stations, local business booths, and an exhibition basketball game. The facility is host to a variety of community activities that previously could not be offered to an underserved community. In addition to an active basketball and volleyball schedule, other activities include dance classes, karate, gymnastics, and performing arts. This project is truly an example of the architect giving form to the peoples' vision in creating a new center at the heart of the community of West Covina.

39

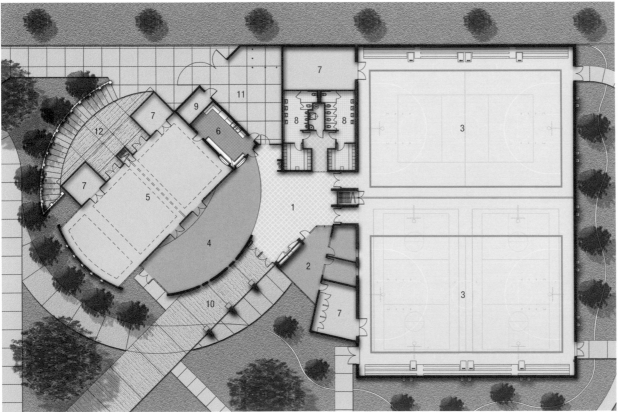

5

1 Lobby
2 Offices
3 Gymnasium
4 Games room
5 Conference room
6 Kitchen
7 Storage
8 Restroom
9 Electrical
10 Patio
11 Entry
12 Service

0   100ft

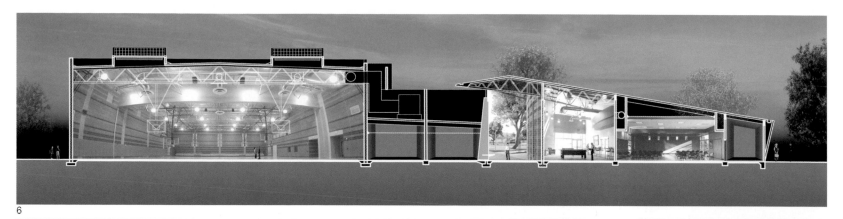

6

7

8

6   A cross-section illustrates the relationship of spaces
7   The youth playroom is fully visible from the front desk
8   A double indoor gymnasium has a dividing wall to accommodate an
    expansion of the basketball and volleyball program
9   The divisible classroom/activity room accommodates a variety of programs
    and has a wood floor for dance and yoga classes
10 The front desk and administrative offices greet the visitor at the entry lobby

9

10

Newport Coast Community Center

Design/Completion 2001/2007

Newport Beach, California

City of Newport Beach

23,700 square feet

Building structure
Concrete masonry gymnasium and wood-framed community center spaces, with exterior plaster and paint, and high-impact interior wallboard; gymnasium roof is tapered steel girders with acoustical metal deck; community center roof is steel girders and wood beams with plywood sheathing and clay barrel tiles

Building materials
Terra cotta barrel roof tiles; exterior cement plaster; custom steel exterior trellis; copper flashing, sheet metal, gutters, and leaders; dark bronze anodized aluminum; high-efficiency glazing; high-efficiency lighting; high recycled content interior materials; water reducing fixtures

The Newport Coast Community Center project began with a financial allocation to create a neighborhood facility as a part of the annexation agreement between Orange County, California and the City of Newport Beach. The Newport Coast community is an Irvine Company development, completing the master plan for the remaining coastal property between Laguna Beach and Newport Beach, California. This primarily residential development is the last significant addition to the established coastal community of Newport Beach. Newport Coast is distinguished by rolling hills and beautiful views of the coastline and valleys of dedicated open space. Residential properties range from high-density apartments and condominiums to expansive homes.

Dougherty + Dougherty was approached to examine potential sites for the promised facility, and to develop a feasibility study for the community center and a potential adjacent branch library. A site was selected on a main intersection at the far end of the Newport Ridge community park. The feasibility study was approved by a resident group, the Newport Coast Advisory Committee, and went before the City Council where the project was approved with a specific request for adequate parking to support significant community events.

The design began with a site development plan that relocated and improved an adjacent playfield, placed the community center with its full gymnasium at the back of the site, and located the library at the corner. The funding limitations resulted in deferring the library or potential community center addition on the corner to a future phase of work. This corner has become a visual extension of open-space park while providing a clear building area for future growth.

The community center facilities respond to the varied needs of the local homeowners' associations and the City of Newport Beach recreational programs. A formal entry lobby provides a gathering area for community events. In addition to a reception counter and lounge area, a computer is available to the public to register for

1

1 The front entry is designed to relate to a future branch library addition
2 The entry plaza is large enough to provide for outdoor gathering and event registration

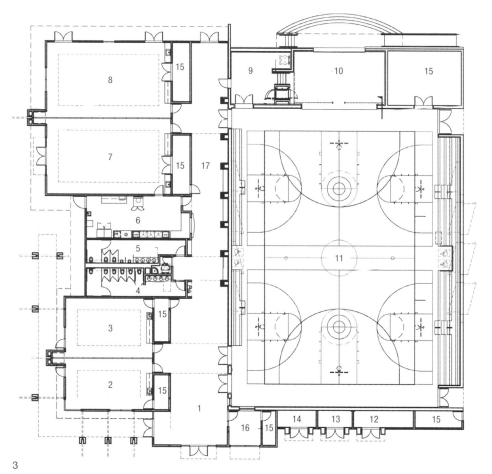

3

1 Lobby/reception	10 Platform
2 Community room 1A	11 Gymnasium
3 Community room 1B	12 Electrical
4 Women's toilets	13 Data
5 Men's toilets	14 Mechanical equipment room
6 Warming kitchen	15 Storage
7 Community room 2	16 Office
8 Community room 3	17 Gallery
9 Wardrobe	

4

3   Floor plan
4   The gymnasium and stage supports recreational programs
     and provides joint-use opportunities for large events

classes or to order books through a library concierge service. Behind the reception desk is an administrative office and storage area for recreational staff.

A full size indoor gymnasium is host to a variety of sporting events and activities. Significant storage areas house sports equipment and portable meeting room furniture. A raised stage, green room, and perimeter acoustical treatment allows the gymnasium to be used for large homeowners' meetings, grand city events, and performances to support local school and community theater arts programs. The stage also opens at the back to an outdoor raised platform and event area.

Two meeting/activity rooms, one large and one smaller, are each divisible with moveable partitions to create four independent rooms to house meeting and recreational activities. A catering kitchen is available to support events, and opens up to a trellised patio where a coffee cart serves bistro-style snacks. A counter facing the lobby corridor offers the opportunity for a concession during sporting events.

Aesthetically, the Newport Coast Community Center is designed to reflect the Mediterranean style, materials and color of the surrounding community, while distinguishing this building as a public gathering place. It enjoys a wealth of Southern California sunshine, with many outdoor opportunities designed for year-round activities in and around the center, and at the adjacent park.

Design strategies include sustainable design considerations, such as the north/south orientation of the building, the use of planting and trellises for sun shading, supplemental thermal and acoustical insulation, high-performance glazing, light shelves for natural lighting, energy-efficient lighting and forced air systems, water efficient fixtures, local materials with recycled

5

6

content, and site stormwater management. Although the city chose not to pursue LEED certification, the building is consistent with the implementation of LEED strategies, short of commissioning during construction.

Predictably, the Newport Coast Community Center is host to more than 200 programs that include Tiny Tot classes, teen after-school activities, adult drop-in basketball, and senior events. It is the largest and most comprehensive municipal recreation facility within the City of Newport Beach, and is home to the many community associations within the Newport Coast neighborhoods. The facility provides a focal point for all residents within the newly developed area of Newport Coast, and is a valued asset complementing life in beautiful Newport Beach.

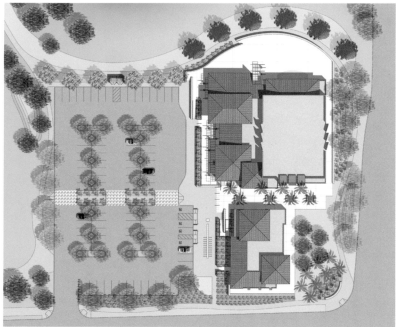

7

5   The hilltop location offers beautiful views of the distant snow-capped Southern California mountain range
6   The lobby provides oversight, registration, waiting areas, and gathering space
7   A site plan orients the community center and future branch library

Crozier Middle School

Design/Completion 2002/2006

Inglewood, California

Inglewood Unified School District

105,000 square feet

Building structure
Concrete slab on grade, steel frame and steel studs, steel deck for second floor and roof

Building materials
Metal siding, high-impact stucco exterior, exterior concrete masonry, high-performance dual glazing

When the Inglewood Unified School District approached Dougherty + Dougherty to modernize Crozier Middle School, the facilities were in total disrepair. This site, home to the first Inglewood school, had sentimental value. A 1950s façade and well-constructed 550-seat auditorium were important assets. Otherwise, the campus was poorly planned, creating areas hidden from view and subject to vandalism. Old buildings suffered serious structural problems. Turf playing fields were nonexistent.

The site was so problematic, we began a year-long effort to obtain state funding for the $28-million replacement project. There was an opportunity for Crozier to be reborn—to restore the auditorium theater, create a new school, rejuvenate open spaces, and establish a new playfield. Staff and community members participated in workshops to define the new Crozier. Two years later, those old buildings came down.

The primary concept for the design of Crozier Middle School organizes areas of access, safety and security, circulation within the site, supportive adjacencies, and simplicity. The plan locates the primary site entrance between the administration building and library. Oversight is addressed through building configurations, clear site lines, and teacher workroom vantage points.

The new campus includes a total of 104,000 square feet for 1300 students in a program that balances art with science, math, and technology. The campus aesthetic reflects the surrounding civic center and is respectful of young adults. The main entrance leads into the two-story administration building and adjacent learning resource and technology center. To the west are two two-story classroom wings and an adjacent two-story art, science, and mathematics lab wing. The cornerstone of the campus is the original auditorium, which has been restored to support school and community theater, and public events.

Environmental techniques address sustainability goals and isolate the building interiors from airplane noise generated by the overhead flight path to Los Angeles

1

1   The rear of the gymnasium building provides an outdoor stage opening and projection wall for amphitheater gatherings and events
2   The primary entrance to Crozier Middle School

1	Arts	19	Health office
2	Attendance staff	20	Kitchen
3	Audience area	21	Lab prep.
4	Audio visual	22	Librarian
5	Band room	23	Listening lab
6	Boys' locker room	24	Lobby
7	Check-out area	25	Office area
8	Classroom	26	Periodical storage
9	Coach's office	27	Practice room
10	Concessions	28	Principal
11	Conference	29	Science lab
12	Consolidated office	30	Stage
13	Corridor	31	Teachers' workroom
14	Counselor	32	Textbook storage
15	Gallery	33	Ticket booth
16	General library area	34	Toilet room
17	Girls' locker room	35	Vice principal
18	Gym/multipurpose	36	Outdoor amphitheater

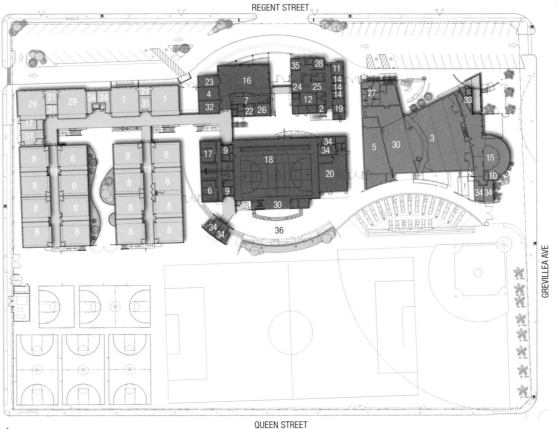

4

3

5

International Airport. Masonry provides durability, sustainability, and increased thermal performance. Post-consumer content is in toilet partitions, tile, and resilient flooring. Plumbing fixtures are low-flow, and light fixtures are energy-efficient fluorescent with sensors. The site is enhanced by a combination of wireless and hardwired telecommunication systems.

The design solution carefully utilizes precious real estate to provide a safe, secure, and supportive environment for a magnet curriculum to maximize learning. The goal is to lead, to instruct, and to empower students to succeed in school and in life. The new school site is the only campus to meet enrollment projections. Within the first academic year test scores increased more than 40 percent.

3   Crozier houses 1300 middle school students on a 7-acre inner-city site
4   A composite site plan/first floor plan illustrating the new design, retaining the original performing arts building
5   The front elevation of the Crozier gymnasium is designed for future mural art
6   Students depart through the main gated entry

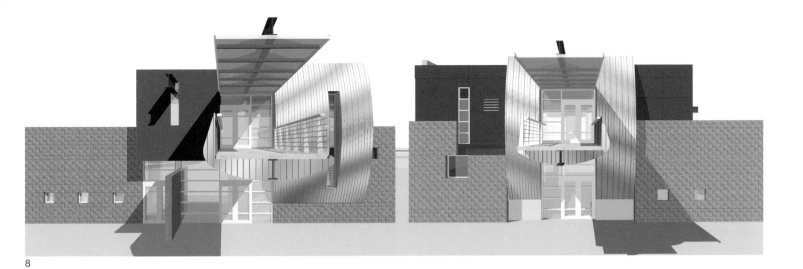

8

7   Forms reflect material applications
8   A perspective rendering showing two different views of a section through the bridge between the library and administrative buildings
9   Circulation between buildings is designed for safe and well-supervised paths of pedestrian travel
10 Forms and details are simple and playful, respectful of the surrounding municipal context

9

10

11

11   A typical classroom
12   The circulation desk for the library/learning resource center
13   A science laboratory classroom

12

13

La Tijera
K–8 School

Design/Completion 2003/2010

Inglewood, California

Inglewood Unified School

63,000 square feet

Building structure
Concrete slab on grade, steel frame
and steel studs, steel deck for second
floor and roof

Building materials
Metal siding, high-impact stucco
exterior, exterior concrete masonry,
high-performance dual glazing

The urban fabric of Los Angeles is mirrored in microcosm on the La Tijera School site, sitting at the nexus of La Cienega Boulevard, a major north–south arterial street, and La Tijera Boulevard. Planes landing at Los Angeles International Airport descend just to the south. Across the street is the landmark "Googie" restaurant, Pann's. Wedged between a culturally diverse neighborhood to the east and the rolling oil fields of old Los Angeles to the north, the site is a jumble of noise, energy, culture, and motion; all of the basic elements of the LA chemistry.

The school sits on a triangular 7-acre sloping site on a major arterial street separating the City of Inglewood from the City of Los Angeles. Multiple jurisdictions, a significant utility setback and dramatic grade changes have all contributed to this challenging site. The success of this project has involved not only design but working as a community advocate in obtaining funding from the State of California for design and construction. State Hardship Replacement Funding has been successfully granted to replace former failing structures built upon old non-compacted fill. The design solution reconceived the old campus, two grade levels with ramps, steps, and elevators serving three levels.

As an urban site there is tension between the need for traffic calming and the need for student recreation space. The old school site accommodated 40 cars and had no off-street drop-off area. The new site plan includes off-street parking for 90 cars and multiple drop-off areas for the main entrance and the kindergarten entrance. This is matched with a plan that more effectively uses the site through multi-story construction freeing up more open space for the students and the community.

The visitor first approaches the administration building or separate kindergarten building with dedicated play area. Beyond the administration building is a gymnasium, locker room and kitchen building with classrooms above and a covered lunch shelter attached. This building is located and designed for community access at other than school hours, giving back a much-needed asset to the citizens. Internal to the site is a two-story

1

1   The design of La Tijera School responds to a sloping site that
    provides the opportunity for a multi-level design solution that
    retains the scale of the surrounding residential community
2   The site plan indicates the limited amount of usable space for
    school activities, and the orientation of the library, gymnasium,
    and playfields for community use
3   The south face of the library/classroom building is protected
    by sun and noise while providing a secondary site entrance
    for library and lower-grade classroom access

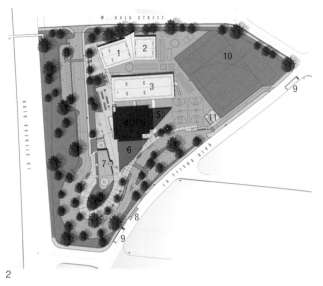

classroom and laboratory building, and single-story classroom buildings beyond. A library designed for public access is tucked under one of these classroom buildings, and is accessible at a lower level where the unstable fill has been removed.

The layered cladding of the La Tijera buildings provides covered walkways and thermal and acoustic protection from the automobile traffic to the south. Environmental design strategies meet the goals of the Collaborative for High Performance Schools program, increasing long-term building performance and lowering maintenance and operations costs. The La Tijera K–8 School is destined to become a focal point for academic excellence and community activities.

1	Classrooms (building L1)
2	Classrooms (building L2)
3	Classrooms (building C)
4	Gymnasium (building G)
5	Lunch shelter
6	Administration (building A)
7	Kindergarten (building K)
8	Charter school bus stop
9	City bus stop
10	Turf playfield
11	Trash and utility enclosure

2

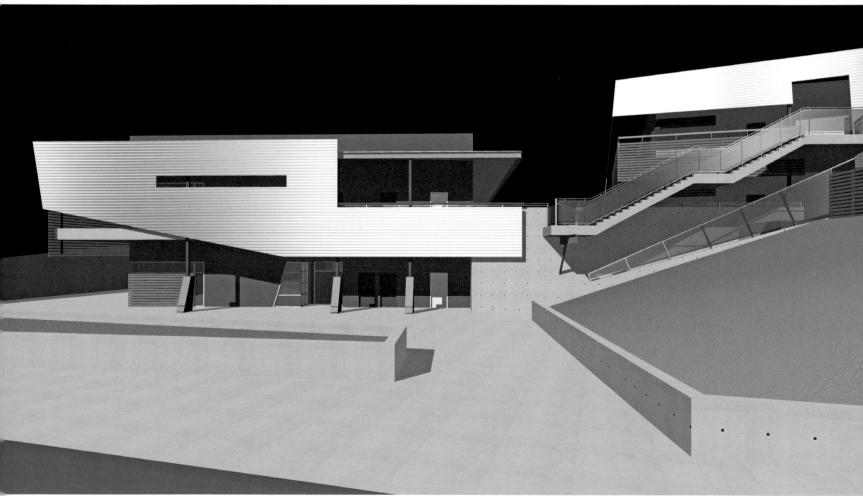

3

Walker Elementary School

Design/Completion 1988/1993

Santa Ana, California

Santa Ana Unified School District

42,000 square feet

Building structure
Structural steel frame with metal decking on conventional concrete spread footings

Building materials
Exterior painted plaster with standing seam metal roof, steel and wood arbors and covered walkways, poured concrete and concrete masonry loggias and site walls

The embrace and shelter of a central courtyard creates the heart of this campus in the urban fabric of Santa Ana. A sense of community runs through each element of this carefully balanced setting. The academic and shared spaces cluster around the courtyard with shaded loggias along the perimeter. On hot days of bright Southern California sun the covered elements provide a "front porch" for the student activities that flow in and around the space.

As you enter the courtyard the central campanile draws you in and looks over all entering, giving a sense of place in an otherwise anonymous neighborhood. The arc of freestanding columns and the yin and yang of the raised and lowered elements give subtle clues to the students and staff about the meaning of place and interaction. It is a canvas for the energy of all who inhabit its enclosure. At times there are colorful banners strung from all of the columns and overhangs trumpeting to the students in the same way that a village festival might lift the spirits of all its inhabitants. At other times the bare concrete elements feel almost Zen-like—on a gray and slightly overcast day they buffer the students from the noise and congestion of the streets just outside. The bridge and the balcony surrounding the central tower provide an area for the students to address their friends in the courtyard below, make speeches in the tradition of the democratic process, or simply rise above the crowd if only for a moment, each one made to feel special.

Located in south Santa Ana, Walker Elementary School is designed to house students on a multi-track year-round calendar. The site includes two multi-story classroom buildings, a multipurpose media center/community room, administrative offices, food service, and a kindergarten complex. The kindergarten has been designed to accommodate child care for general use by the community. The classrooms and media center have all been networked for data, video, and communication. Community input and needs have been integrated into the design through the development and placement of the playing fields,

1   The street entrance to Adeline Walker Elementary School leads to a symmetrical courtyard bordered by the administration building and the community/multipurpose/library building
2   Circulation space is defined by handrails and outdoor covered walkways that become screens and overhangs for the shading of south-facing walls

1

3

4

access to the media center for community meetings, and the design of the central plaza for both school and community functions.

Mindful of resource conservation, the design provides specially designed sun shading on the south-facing windows and walls—overhanging covered walkways that both shelter the students and shade the building. Energy-efficient HVAC and lighting systems reduce consumption. Shared spaces provide more effective use of the available space to reduce the building's footprint. Natural light and ventilation are available to all of the spaces to provide comfort as well as a connection between the students and teachers and the surrounding environment.

5

3   The hardscape courtyard provides an amphitheater for outdoor classes and campus gatherings
4   Classrooms offer options for lighting, extensive lockable cabinets, marker boards and tack boards, and acoustic treatment for enhanced high-performance teaching space
5   The administration building's lobby is playful in its simplicity

Education Operation Support Center

Design/Completion 2003/2010

Ventura, California

Ventura Unified School District

37,914 square feet

Building structure
Concrete masonry walls with steel roof structure; conventional concrete footings with concrete slab on grade

Building materials
Exposed concrete masonry walls with translucent insulated panels; flexible photovoltaic system integrated into roofing membrane, high-efficiency lighting and HVAC systems; pervious paving materials throughout the site, use of drought tolerant native plants with water saving features throughout; high recycled content materials in all areas of project

The west side of the City of Ventura has been a tangle of industrial, commercial, and sporadic residential development laced with the remnants of citrus groves and historic cultural elements for over a century. This area was once the home to a thriving Hispanic population. Redevelopment during the early part of the 1900s displaced these original settlers and left a vacuum waiting to be filled. The newly constructed freeway allowed easy access for manufacturing and soon the streets were filled with the sound of steel and engines. As the infrastructure aged, large tracts began to decay and secondary uses filled in the gaps. Stanley Avenue, the key link between the nearby freeway and the main arterial was seen as the primary element to revitalize this valuable community fabric. The city developed a vision and invested in the public infrastructure to "kick start" the process.

While the city's vision was taking form, The Ventura Unified School District acquired a major portion of the property along Stanley Avenue, giving rise to the opportunity for a partnership between the city and the schools. In need of a centralized location for its widely dispersed district support operations the district acquired the old vacant Kinko's headquarters including a broad empty asphalt lot that fronted Stanley Avenue. The vision was to create a new facility on this site that would house maintenance and operations functions, the district warehouse as well as a bus maintenance facility. The key was to design this in a way that was an uplifting front door for the district administrative offices already located to the north of the site as well as the first link in the city's plan for the west side of Ventura.

Knowing that how this new facility embraced its street edge would ultimately be its key to success, the design of the new EOSC uses the street frontage to provide a public amenity and thus a sense of community for all who pass by. The edge is bordered by an articulated wall that creates alcoves for sitting along the street frontage, trees, pockets of indigenous plants, and an inviting streetscape that offers life to this previously hostile environment. The corner of the facility is both

1

1   The new building is the first to establish a street life in this
      transitional industrial neighborhood
2   The building entrance conveys the nature of the activities within

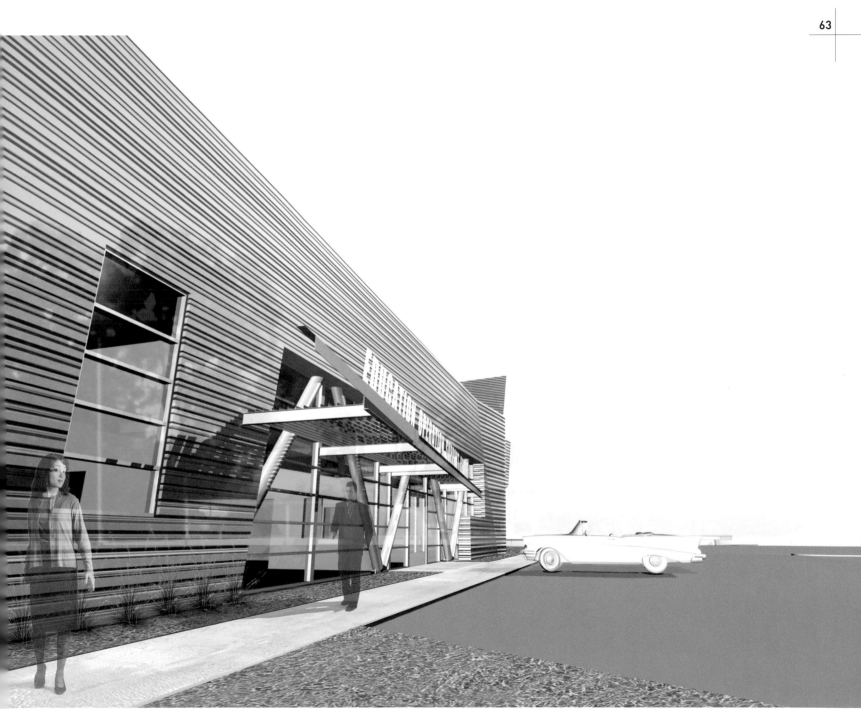

3

4

5

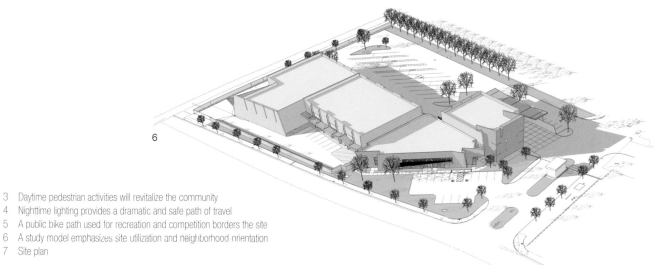

3   Daytime pedestrian activities will revitalize the community
4   Nighttime lighting provides a dramatic and safe path of travel
5   A public bike path used for recreation and competition borders the site
6   A study model emphasizes site utilization and neighborhood orientation
7   Site plan

1   Education Operation Support Center
2   Existing VUSD Administration Facility
3   Existing vegetation
4   Bus parking
5   Bus wash
6   Entrance gate
7   Guard house

a parking area for access to the administrative offices and a plaza of enriched paving and canopy trees that opens to the public for weekend gatherings. The west side of the center provides a newly landscaped edge to enhance the adjacent river bike trail. Careful attention has been placed on utilizing native plants and water reducing landscape to serve as an example to the community regarding stewardship of the environment.

The building is both visually striking and an example of optimal resource efficiency. Designed to a LEED Silver standard, the building incorporates natural daylighting and ventilation, energy-efficient lighting and HVAC systems, water-saving plumbing systems, photovoltaics and high recycled content materials throughout. The site was selected because of its previous use as an abandoned industrial facility and its proximity to both public transit and the community bike trail system. Alternative fuels are provided on-site for the district buses and waste materials are recycled in an active on-site program.

The success of this new asset for the Ventura Unified School District is in the partnership it creates with the community and the long-term enhancement of the district resources through effective centralization of operations. The urban fabric of the City of Ventura will be re-energized by this thoughtful and considered development in the realization of the new vision for the west side of the community.

7

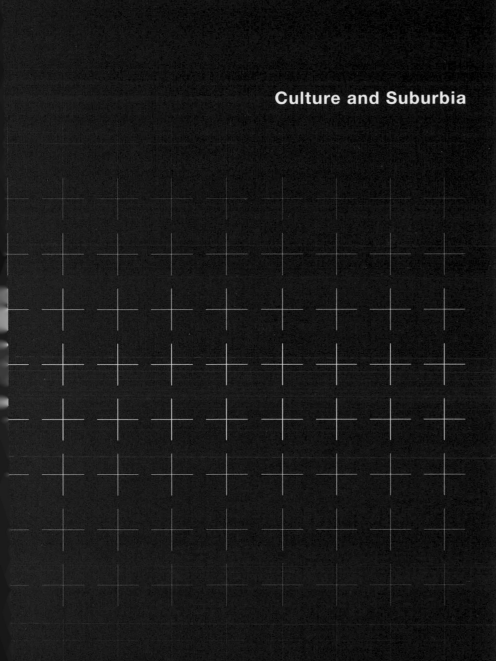

Culture and Suburbia

Neither here nor there, suburbia, edge city, sprawl; those living 'in between' often feel a longing to find the cultural experience we all crave to construct a satisfying life. This void can be all consuming. It is partially a result of age, texture, and an absence of the diversity that creates the richness we embrace to fulfill our spiritual universe. In this ocean of rolling lawns, islands of trees, and beige and gray stucco how do we create the icons that will define our future history? *Webster's Dictionary* defines culture as the integrated pattern of human knowledge, belief, and behavior that depends upon the capacity for learning and transmitting knowledge to succeeding generations. It is further stated that culture is the customary beliefs, social forms, and material traits of a racial, religious, or social group. If suburbia is a place we are all new to, how then can we infuse this existence with the history and substance of culture that we crave and need?

We must look for the subtle clues that are lying beneath the surface of this place. What was here before the houses? What remains from that recent past? Ghosts do exist: of previous cultures and the footprints they left for us to follow; of distant mountains that cast shadows and teach us how our predecessors lived on these plains. Patterns of settlement intersect in ways that allow us to establish a new path. Within the avenues of ancestral travel are the notes that guide us in creating the new cultural plazas. We will teach our children the history of this new place. A column rising in a field defines itself in relationship to all of the surrounding elements. At the same time it redefines all that surrounds it by offering a new vantage point, a node from which to measure distance, a point to gather around, to share, to teach. Color draws in the eye, speaks to culture and time. It is a reflection of shared joy and sorrow. Our buildings tell stories and evoke memories that will transmit knowledge from generation to generation. This is the seed that is planted from which a new culture will grow and flourish.

The opportunity to design an island of culture in an ocean of the suburban landscape was the inspiration. Built in the 1960s, Thousand Oaks High School had originally been planned with the concept of providing a community performing arts center in mind. The land had been set aside on the campus and had been carefully protected from the pressures of academic development for decades. Infrastructure was routed around the site; new buildings were kept at bay, all with the deep commitment that this would one day provide a place for students and community to house their artistic aspirations.

The design process was one of getting past the deep skepticism that had been generated by years of near-miss activity. The community and staff maintained a "we'll believe it when we see it" approach. But the ideas that had fermented for all of those decades were strong. This was to be jointly funded by the school and the city and, as such, needed to be open to both. It would be a landmark building, but needed to complement the existing campus fabric rather than stand against it. It needed the flexibility to house musical comedies as well as lectures. It needed space for drama and for assembly. It also needed to provide a bridge between the visual and the performing arts.

The new performing arts center provides both a physical and philosophical link to the surrounding community. Situated on the most prominent corner of the campus, this 400-seat facility opens to the public for evening and weekend performances, serving the campus and student body during the week. The state-of-the-art theater provides a setting for curriculum in dramatic arts and music with a full fly loft and stage, dressing space, high-tech control systems, and support facilities. The lobby, with its radiating beams, reaches out to the passing community and beckons them to come inside. The glass of the lobby echoes the transparency of the public forum that is the underpinning of the performing arts. Large display areas provide gallery space for the exhibition of student artwork.

1 A formal entrance hosts large audiences
2 The ticket office draws the queue away from the entry

Thousand Oaks High School Performing Arts Center

Design/Completion 1994/1999

Thousand Oaks, California

Conejo Valley Unified School District

10,500 square feet

Building structure
Steel frame with lightweight steel truss roof

Building materials
Plaster exterior with high-performance glazing in steel frames, interior exposed concrete floors, recycled-content carpeting in limited areas, ceramic tile and fabrics for seating are high recycled content, low-VOC finishes throughout

1

2

4

Sustainability is an integral element of the design. Natural light from the rising sun fills the lobby, non-toxic materials are utilized throughout, energy-efficient systems control the environment, and computers link each element for optimization. The new center is an asset that will provide the opportunity for students and the community to explore the world of the performing arts together for the coming generations.

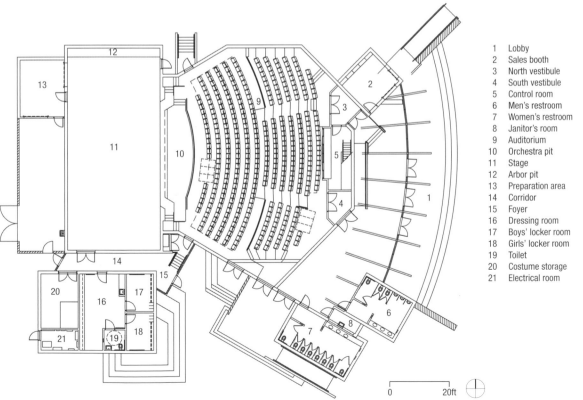

5

1	Lobby
2	Sales booth
3	North vestibule
4	South vestibule
5	Control room
6	Men's restroom
7	Women's restroom
8	Janitor's room
9	Auditorium
10	Orchestra pit
11	Stage
12	Arbor pit
13	Preparation area
14	Corridor
15	Foyer
16	Dressing room
17	Boys' locker room
18	Girls' locker room
19	Toilet
20	Costume storage
21	Electrical room

0   20ft

In Culver City, a suburb of Los Angeles, the atmosphere is pervaded by a long history of motion pictures. The former MGM Studios (now Sony) loom over shops and restaurants of downtown Culver City. The old Culver Studios—the location for the filming of classic films such as *Gone with the Wind*—are just around the corner. With this energy woven into the fabric of Culver City it is only natural that the High School should have a core interest in the visual and performing arts. Until the design of the new photo and video lab for the 1950s campus there was little room dedicated to this vital element of the community's culture.

The high-tech fine arts photo lab building defines a new edge along the south perimeter of the campus. Prior to the creation of this space, the campus seemed to bleed into the adjacent athletic fields without regard for visual or cultural identity. A core element of the program was to define both the exterior as a gathering place for artistic talent and the interior as a canvas for the honing of skills that could later be carried into careers within the entertainment industry. With its sweeping metal trellises, the courtyard of the photo lab is the node for activity at this side of the campus. Students gather to share their latest projects and friends meet to simply connect and catch up.

The buildings themselves provide a backdrop that can be utilized as stage setting and inspirational form. The campus axes join at this point and enforce an existing circulation spine with a well-defined amphitheater for outdoor teaching. Building forms, materials, and colors all reflect the patterns established within the existing campus, reflecting the sloped walls of the original buildings of the 1950s. It is at once contemporary and "retro." Views to the fields beyond are now framed with narrow canyon passages from the courtyard and energy is directed along the south edge of the campus from the photo lab to the adjacent athletic buildings to the east. This provides a continuous link between activity spaces that reinforces the spirit and camaraderie of campus life.

1   The vestibules signify the individual entrances to the studio spaces
2   The photo-lab addition creates an outdoor gathering space as a
    focal point, giving meaning to the existing site circulation pattern

Culver City High School Photo Lab Classroom Addition

Design/Completion 1999/2002
Culver City, California
Culver City Unified School District
6500 square feet

Building structure
Light steel framing with wood infill framing; wood roof with conventional concrete footings

Building materials
Exterior plaster, high-efficiency glazing, high insulation of the building shell for energy conservation, high-efficiency lighting and HVAC systems with natural light and ventilation, high recycled content interior materials, water reducing fixtures

1

3 The classroom building and photo lab building come together to create a gateway through the campus
4 Floor plan
5 Vestibules protrude from the façade to signify points of entry to the studio
6 The circular form of the building reaches out to capture space and define its relationship to adjacent facilities
7 The interior of the photography studio supports a unique high school curriculum for the arts
8 Site sketch
9 The photo lab supports traditional film processing and printing as well as digital media production and editing

1 Photo studio classroom
2 Classroom
3 Storage
4 Darkroom
5 Bathrooms
6 Courtyard
7 Existing classroom

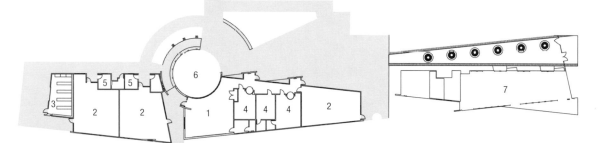

4

3

5

6

7

The Culver City location offers a unique opportunity to support a partnership with the local film industry. Few school districts offer a state-of-the-art photo studio with classroom, darkroom, and studio space. It is anticipated that the graduates of this unique elective program will become the future of the film industry.

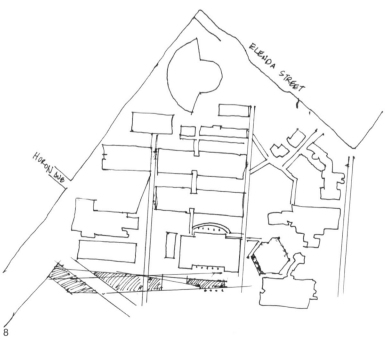

8

9

California State University, Dominguez Hills – Extended Education Campus

Design/Completion 1997/2000

Carson, California

California State University, Dominguez Hills

25,000 square feet

Building structure
Concrete masonry walls, steel frame, metal deck, and metal roofing

Building materials
Exposed concrete masonry, exposed steel-framed roof/ceiling, metal canopies and metal roofing, high-performance glazing in aluminum window walls

Creating an educational facility that will serve and expand a diverse population of students in a flexible setting is the basis for the design of this unique facility. Drawing from high school students, college-age students, and working adults, this project is a contemporary community asset. The facility provides distance-learning opportunities to link the Dominguez Hills campus with other institutions of higher learning. It provides a connection between the academic buildings and the proposed adjacent Staples Sports Complex. The front points of entry address adjacent pedestrian and vehicular paths of travel. The placement of the buildings defines the edge of campus where adjacent public sports venues meet academic buildings, with community and student-body access to both.

The new building provides administrative office space, a registration building, a conferencing center available to on-campus and off-campus groups, and high-tech instructional classrooms and lecture halls. A collection of three buildings segregates uses to allow independent operating hours, and evening and weekend class schedules. The spaces between buildings provide opportunities for outdoor events and outdoor teaching settings. An executive conference room has an attached serving kitchen, restrooms, and a private outdoor patio for high-level university meetings, and is accessible to the public for lease.

Building design incorporates environmentally responsive solutions for natural and artificial lighting, air distribution systems, and easily maintained and durable building materials. Sustainable strategies include: energy-efficient lighting to supplement the introduction of natural lighting through high-performance glazing and skylights, a central plant for forced air heating and ventilating to multiple buildings, water-efficient plumbing fixtures, a high ratio of pervious exterior surfaces for stormwater retention, water-efficient plant materials, and reclaimed water for irrigation. The project has been independently funded through Extended Education program activities.

1 An assembly of buildings accommodates a lecture hall, classrooms, registration areas, and administrative offices, while enclosing an outdoor courtyard for events
2 The image of the new Extended Education building provides a signature for new centralized adult-education services for the campus

1

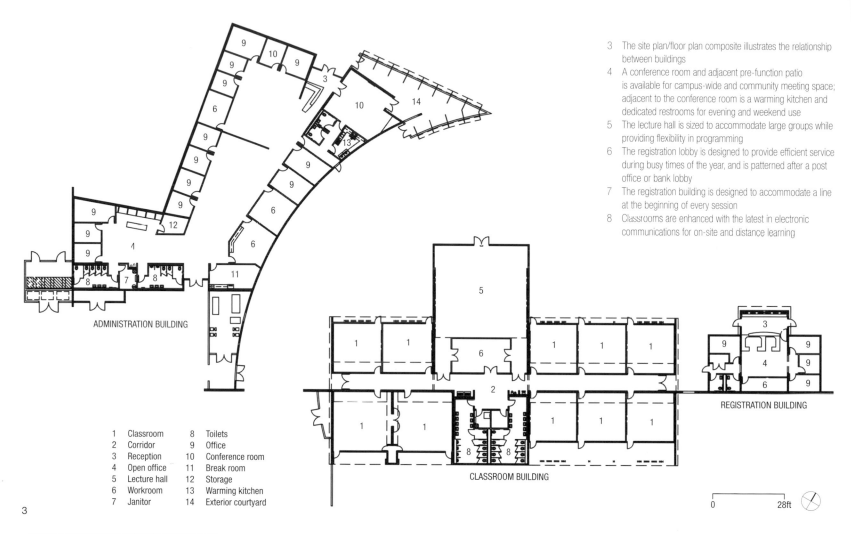

ADMINISTRATION BUILDING

CLASSROOM BUILDING

REGISTRATION BUILDING

3 The site plan/floor plan composite illustrates the relationship between buildings
4 A conference room and adjacent pre-function patio is available for campus-wide and community meeting space; adjacent to the conference room is a warming kitchen and dedicated restrooms for evening and weekend use
5 The lecture hall is sized to accommodate large groups while providing flexibility in programming
6 The registration lobby is designed to provide efficient service during busy times of the year, and is patterned after a post office or bank lobby
7 The registration building is designed to accommodate a line at the beginning of every session
8 Classrooms are enhanced with the latest in electronic communications for on-site and distance learning

1	Classroom	8	Toilets
2	Corridor	9	Office
3	Reception	10	Conference room
4	Open office	11	Break room
5	Lecture hall	12	Storage
6	Workroom	13	Warming kitchen
7	Janitor	14	Exterior courtyard

0   28ft

3

4

5

6

7

8

Building materials are selected for durability and compatibility with existing buildings. Concrete masonry is the predominant exterior and exposed-interior structural and finish material, and is accented with steel structure, canopies, and enclosure walls. Expanses of high-performance glazing enhance light, views, and supervision. Exposed structure expands the perimeter of the building envelope, and adds a high-tech feel to a technology-savvy educational curriculum.

The resulting complex of educational and administrative buildings consolidates the extended education program into its own micro-campus, and provides a home to the greatest income-producing and community-enhancing program offered at the university.

A new residential subdivision in an upscale part of Ventura County near the California coast is the picture of the quintessential suburban neighborhood. New single-family homes surround a vacant 10-acre flat lot with an open meandering park, newly landscaped along its northern border. But there is a need for place, identity, and culture within this embryonic environment. The students want a place that is exciting, identifiable, challenging, but that respects its neighbors. How do you create a "there" when there is no "there?"

Drawing from the subtle cues of the adjacent landscape, views to the distant mountains, prevailing breezes from the Pacific Ocean and the path of the sun as it arcs overhead, the plan for the Rio Del Norte School imagines each of those elements carving its shape into the barren piece of land. The entry to the school and adjacent multipurpose space anchors the campus on the southwest corner, announcing to all that this is a special place where all are welcome and will share in the academic and cultural fabric that is woven within. Surrounding the landscaped courtyard are clusters of classrooms each with a shared technology space at its center that encourages students and teachers to move outside the classroom and to interact with their broader campus community. Outdoor teaching space graces the entry to each of these clusters allowing the classroom setting to reach outside in the idyllic coastal climate. A large amphitheater is the pivotal element of the campus and is balanced at the north end of the courtyard with a shared gardening space and recycling area to teach practical lessons regarding how humankind interacts with nature and connects to resources.

The colors and textures of the campus are reflective of its relationship with the neighborhood. The perimeter walls are muted in color and simple in form, echoing the scale and materials of the surrounding homes. The interior courtyard is an exuberant collection of soaring forms with vibrant colors that reflect the energy and activity of the students and faculty within its embrace. Sharing campus resources is a part of every element.

1 The street elevation borrows form and color from the surrounding neighborhood
2 The multipurpose room stage opens to a centrally located outdoor amphitheater

Rio Del Norte Elementary School

Design/Completion 1997/2001

Oxnard, California

Rio School District

46,000 square feet

Building structure
Wood framed construction with Glulam roof structure; conventional concrete footings

Building materials
Exterior plaster, high-efficiency glazing, natural ventilation and high-efficiency HVAC, natural light in all spaces with high-efficiency lighting; controls are linked to light levels and a district-wide energy management system; high recycled content in all finishes and casework; upgraded insulation to reduce energy consumption; on-site material recycling and urban gardening enhanced with pervious paving materials

1

3 The composite site plan/floor plan expresses the approach to the site development solution, with an axis clearly orienting buildings and functions

4 The central courtyard is defined on the south side by a wayfinding wall

5 Rio del Norte, centrally located within a newly developed residential community, reaches out to welcome families to the new school

6 The classroom clusters, lit by pyramid skylights, march along the edge of the playground

7 The multipurpose room supports activities ranging from mealtime to basketball

8 Classroom interiors benefit from a variety of environmental strategies, including natural light and air circulation

1   Multipurpose
2   Administration
3   PTA room
4   Library/LRC
5   Computer lab
6   Kindergarten
7   Classroom
8   Tech lab
9   Restroom kiosk
10 Amphitheater
11 Courtyard
12 Play area

3

4

5

The multipurpose building is located to allow easy access on weekends and evenings for a multitude of functions. A medical office is located to allow weekend health clinics for parents and friends. Playing fields are available to encourage recreation and athletics, promoting community health and wellness. The successful nurturing of culture in this suburban landscape is best reflected in the number of students enrolled in the school's inaugural year of operation, exceeding projections by nearly 20 percent.

6

7

8

La Mirada High School Classroom Addition

Design/Completion 2003/2007

La Mirada, California

Norwalk La Mirada Unified School District

28,900 square feet

Building structure
Light steel framing with wood infill framing; wood roof with conventional concrete footings

Building materials
Exterior plaster, high-efficiency glazing, high insulation of the building shell for energy conservation, high-efficiency lighting and HVAC systems with natural light and ventilation, high recycled content interior materials and pervious paving on the exterior; water reducing fixtures

The rolling hills of La Mirada are dotted with trees and single-family homes. The nearby golf course is nestled in a small green valley. The local high school campus, designed in the 1960s, is a sprawling plan of single-story buildings that seem to leak out into the surrounding environment. There is no edge, literally or figuratively, to this place. The community was seeking a design that would capture today's culture, provide a place for students to gather, enhance their academic science experience, and create a new edge between the campus and the play fields beyond.

La Mirada High School is distinguished by a tightly packed central campus plan that leaves little room for planned growth within its borders. The new classroom/lab addition replaces myriad re-locatable classrooms that are currently littered around the campus perimeter. The new 28,900-square-foot building provides eight classrooms, four stacked science labs, and two bays for administrative and support space that can be converted into future classrooms. The "imaginary" site perimeter encapsulates 34,000 square feet of building surrounding new outdoor courtyards and gathering places.

The chosen direction hugs the edge of the site, gingerly poking at the inner ring with an undulating concentric curve, which transitions the podium of the existing campus area to the playing fields below. Maintaining vehicular access between buildings and pedestrian access through grade changes has been carefully accommodated and concealed through a succession of courtyards and defined outdoor gathering places. Landscaping shades these courtyards and seating provides a setting that encourages the students to interact with other students. The exchange of ideas is seen as vital to enriching the curriculum of the school and to expanding the discussion of lessons learned within the science labs and lecture rooms. Natural light filters into all of the interior spaces providing an opportunity to reduce energy consumption and a connection between the students and the

1 Classroom pods gingerly march along the north elevation
2 Floor plans
3 A relatively significant two-story building is dematerialized through massing
4 A centrally located stair anchors the plaza linking the new building to the existing campus

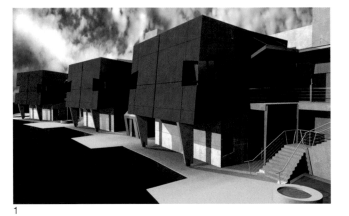

1

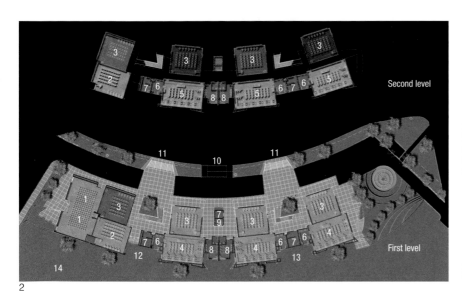

1	Multipurpose room
2	Science lab
3	Classroom
4	Physics lab
5	Chemistry lab
6	Teachers' work lab
7	Mechanical room
8	Restrooms
9	Elevator
10	Existing stair
11	Existing ramp
12	Baseball-field entrance
13	Science planters
14	Baseball fields

Second level

First level

0   75ft

2

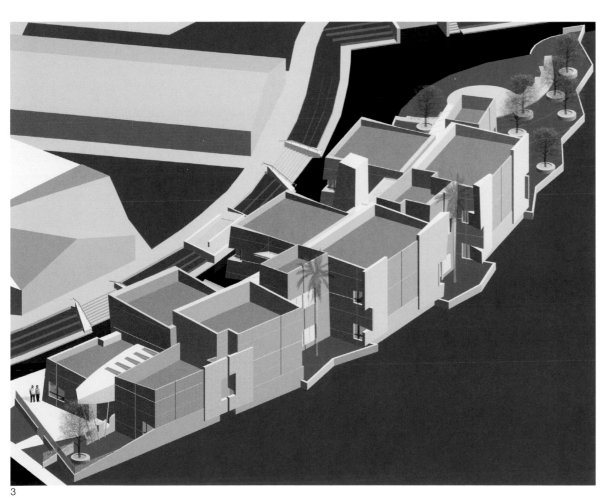

3

4

surrounding hills. The scale of the two-story building has been reduced through the fractured plan and winding circulation corridor. The exterior articulation of the arched façade shades the south face of the building while protecting it from stray foul balls. The result is a fitting but unique contribution to the high school campus, creating flexible yet highly defined classrooms and laboratories to support a district commitment to an aggressive science curriculum. The new addition has become a clearly identifiable icon of the students' passion for learning and the community's cultural enrichment of the next generation.

Youth and Heritage

A dichotomy—we are each in transition, drawing lessons from our childhood and wondering about our place in our lineage. The heritage of each environment is reflected in the buildings we create to house our society, young and old. We explore, engage, gather, and search. Youth is a process of consuming all that is at our fingertips and beyond, transforming these images into the intelligence that informs our heart. Heritage is not a book written with perfect intent. It is slowly revealed as we age. Our youth is the heritage of the next generation. As it is often said, "the child is father to the man." What then separates youth and heritage or, perhaps more importantly, what binds the two? There is no bridge that we gaze across with youth standing on one side wondering about heritage on the other bank. It is more like a series of mirrors on each side of a narrow hallway. We turn from side to side and see our reflection on into infinity, always slightly concealed by our current image.

Our architecture must celebrate the youth and youthfulness of our culture while embracing the wisdom that resides within its heritage. We have the ability to transport each person to a place where they can tap into that energy that flows from the wellspring of the young. The time we find ourselves looking back and walking toward the future is that intersection between youth and heritage. Can we capture this ephemeral spirit through our design? Is it a form that unlocks the memory of something we had left on the playing field when we were small? Is it a color that jogs our emotions and, like the aroma from our childhood kitchen, transports us to another era? Can we bring together generations in a human exchange of youthful energy and aging heritage? Knowledge is perhaps the greatest bridge at the intersection of these two powerful forces. The oral tradition becomes a visual language of building that joins each of us as we hold hands through time.

Tustin Family and Youth Center

Design/Completion 1995/1997

Tustin, California

City of Tustin

6000 square feet

Building structure
Recycled concrete masonry shell with lightweight panelized wood roof

Building materials
Plaster and paint exterior with aluminum window system, energy-efficient glazing, energy-efficient interior lighting systems with low-VOC finishes, water-efficient plumbing fixtures, recycled content in carpet, tile and other finishes

Recycling an old pizza parlor is perhaps the most appropriate metaphor for bridging the generations. Located near an under-served neighborhood school in an abandoned corner commercial storefront and surrounded by an old hospital, the Tustin Family and Youth Center gives new life to this decaying community asset. Envisioned as a link between the generations, the facility gives a home to local children after school to "hang out," do their homework, shoot baskets, and surf the web. Their younger siblings have a Headstart childcare facility that is integrated into the site and offers the opportunity for neighborhood seniors to assist with their supervision and to serve as mentors. It is a "billboard" of bright colors and exuberant shapes at the terminus of a freeway off-ramp and a hub of cultural activity.

Built on a shoestring budget, the center is an overwhelming success. The 6000-square-foot facility maintained the basic shell of the existing strip mall and carved out new childcare areas, meeting rooms, counseling spaces, a computer learning center, administrative offices, and a shared kitchen and workroom. It is constantly busy as children, seniors, and parents come and go to link with the variety of social services provided by the City of Tustin in a single location. Envisioned as a place that would be seen through the eyes of a child or inspire those in their later years to reconnect with their childhood, the shapes and colors of the center bring a smile to all who pass by and invite the casual visitor to come in and explore what might be going on inside. Activities spill from the walls to the front parking lot where a basketball court occupies the space after the cars and rush of parents dropping off their children in the morning subside.

Always mindful of the long-term benefits of thinking green, Dougherty + Dougherty created a design infused with low-cost environmental concepts such as water- and energy-efficient equipment, doubling and tripling the programmable uses for each space, low-VOC materials with high recycled content and the basic underpinning of recycling the entire structural shell of the building.

1

1 The relationship between color and form represents the activities within
2 The existing building had been abandoned for several years
3 The new youth center is a perfect example of adaptive re-use

2

3

1 Lobby
2 Meeting
3 Lounge
4 Computer
5 Women's restroom
6 Men's restroom
7 Laundry
8 Toilet
9 Classroom
10 Office
11 Nurse
12 Staff workroom
13 Counseling
14 Janitor
15 Kitchen
16 Pantry
17 Storage

NEW PARKING

0   16ft

4

6

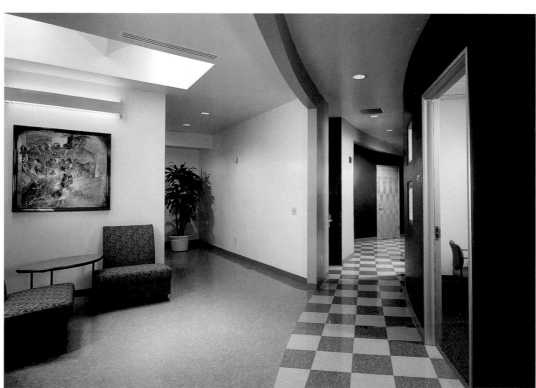

5

4 The floor plan is a simple reinvention of the existing building
5 The circular path connects a variety of community services
6 The interior prior to the renovation
7 A portion of the old existing parking area is now a playground
8 The pre-school classrooms emphasize fun

7

8

Garfield Elementary School

Design/Completion 1987/1991

Santa Ana, California

Santa Ana Unified School District

42,000 square feet

Building structure
Structural steel frame with metal decking on conventional concrete spread footings

Building materials
Exterior painted plaster with standing seam metal roof; steel and wood arbors and covered walkways; concrete masonry loggias and site walls

Garfield Elementary School was conceived as a children's village where the architecture reflected lessons about ideas, collaboration, pride, and culture. The small 4-acre site is carved from a densely populated neighborhood—the land was made available by the demolition of old industrial and commercial properties. The dilemma we faced with our client included the reality that any land we utilized to create this school was going to displace a number of the students for whom the facility was being designed. The result was a heightened consciousness about creating a community asset that offered support to the students at all times and that could have multiple uses. When completed, the play yard would represent the only open space in this crowded environment. It was to be a precious commodity that would be treasured by the children, their parents, and the community.

The plan of the school places the library and multipurpose building at the center of the campus. This symbolizes the importance of access to knowledge in a democratic setting. The axial plan proceeds from the entry court, flanked by the administration building and the two-story classroom wing. The elevator tower with its large clock highlights the ceremonial entrance to the village and the significance of the library. With space at such a premium, every square foot of land was preserved and its use maximized to offer the optimal resource for the students and the neighborhood. The back of the library provides an outdoor stage and grassy gathering court. The adjacent lunch shelter extends this open space and provides an exterior assembly space for both school and community gatherings.

Among the clutter of the myriad derelict buildings on the site prior to demolition, it was discovered that a historic old Pacific Red Car power generating station occupied one corner of the school site. This potential impediment was instead seen as an opportunity. The beautiful small gem of a brick building was restored and planned for conversion to a district testing facility and as a community resource to provide a stronger link between the school district and its constituents.

1　The street entrance integrates the pedestrian and vehicular entrances to the site to orient the visitor toward the administration building to the right, the centrally located multipurpose/library building, and the two-story classroom building to the left

2　The main entrance to Garfield Elementary School welcomes visitors with the multipurpose/library building as a colorful focal point

1

4

3

5

Garfield Elementary School accommodates 780 students on a multi-track, year-round basis. Knowing that open space would always be at a premium, half of the site was preserved as recreational space and the other half dedicated to academic activities. The linked courtyards and loggias with formal planting provide a tranquil setting for reflection in a chaotic urban setting. Careful material and infrastructure selection provides both an uplifting and enlightened environment as well as a resource-efficient asset for the client.

6

3   The stairway to the second floor of the classroom building doubles as an outdoor classroom and gathering place
4   The covered lunch area and courtyard between buildings supports school activities as well as after-school community programs
5   The classrooms are designed to provide a variety of lighting levels and provide secure storage for multi-track programs
6   The administration lobby is a colorful extension of the design vocabulary

Lucille Smith
Elementary School

Design/Completion 2001/2006

Lawndale, California

Lawndale Elementary School District

35,376 square feet

Building structure
Concrete slab-on-grade, wood frame,
stucco walls, built-up roof

Building materials
Simple cost-effective stucco exterior
walls, built-up roof; interior materials
include: gypsum board and
tackable/acoustical wall covering,
unique floors, tile restroom floors and
walls, suspended acoustical ceilings

Lucille Smith Elementary School represents the rebirth of an old school on an existing site. The former small campus had been leased out and had fallen into a state of disrepair. The existing buildings were demolished and an adjacent small parcel of church land was acquired to accommodate a new high-density, K-5 campus on a 3-acre flat urban site. It was important to re-establish this public school as a focal point within the civic center and to respect the significance that the school maintained as a center of neighborhood activity and community culture. The original bell that rang in the former church is mounted next to the school flagpole at the entrance to the campus.

The administration wing and principal's office oversee the campus entrance. An adjacent entrance serves a new dedicated kindergarten classroom building and a secure play area. A nurse's station, teachers' workroom, and lounge complement the administrative offices. A multipurpose room is enhanced with a stage for school and community events, as well as drop down tables for dining. At the rear of the multipurpose room is the library, separated by a moveable partition for the potential expansion of either space to accommodate a variety of activities. Adjacent to the multipurpose room are a serving kitchen and a covered outdoor lunch shelter. The two-story classroom building provides remote teacher workrooms and two first-floor classrooms that are sized to accommodate kindergarten classes depending upon enrollment. Classrooms are enhanced with tackable/acoustical wall covering throughout, learning walls with moveable white boards, storage and television cabinets, technology interface, and natural light and ventilation.

The carefully articulated spaces between buildings provide for a joint-use outdoor amphitheater, a kindergarten play area, a courtyard within the classroom building, and access to an elementary-scaled hard-court play area and play field. Form and color define these spaces, and emphasize the playful nature of this inner-city home for the children of Lawndale.

1

1   A central courtyard facilitates circulation through the site while providing an outdoor amphitheater to accommodate the entire student population as well as hosting community events
2   Colonnade details provide sun shading and covered walkways
3   The front of the school provides secure oversight for elementary and kindergarten students

2

3

4

5

4   The kindergarten play area secures a corner
    of the site for as many as four kindergarten
    classrooms
5   A typical classroom is washed with natural
    light, is wrapped with tackable acoustical
    wall covering, and provides a teaching wall
    with storage and rolling marker boards
6   The multipurpose room includes a stage
    and drop-down lunch tables
7   Site plan
8   The library includes a computer room, and
    a moveable wall and moveable shelving to
    provide overflow seating for the
    multipurpose room

6

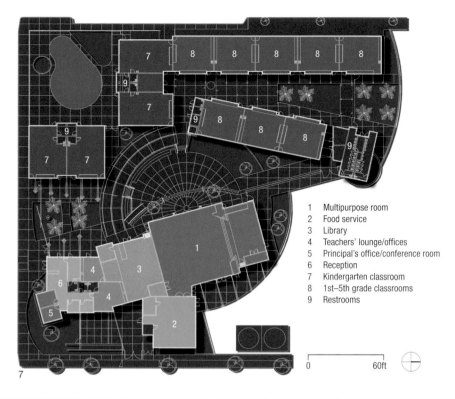

1 Multipurpose room
2 Food service
3 Library
4 Teachers' lounge/offices
5 Principal's office/conference room
6 Reception
7 Kindergarten classroom
8 1st–5th grade classrooms
9 Restrooms

0   60ft

7

8

Los Angeles Mission College Library and Learning Resource Center

Design/Completion 1993/1997

Sylmar, California

Los Angeles Mission College

77,000 square feet

Building structure
Poured in-place concrete retaining walls for the semi-subterranean building areas; braced steel frame with steel deck for above grade areas

Building materials
Exterior plaster walls, clay tile roof, aluminum curtain wall and storefront windows with high-efficiency glazing, high recycled content materials throughout, energy efficient lighting systems, under-floor accessible electrical ducts for flexibility, rotary cut birch; high-efficiency gas absorption HVAC system with supplemental funding from the local utility

Sylmar is a proud community in the extreme northwest corner of the San Fernando Valley. Often thought of as a suburb of Los Angeles, it has its own heritage and sense of place. Set against the backdrop of the towering San Gabriel Mountains rising to the north, it is perhaps best known internationally as the epicenter of several major earthquakes. It is also buffeted by hostile Santa Ana winds, which can reach hurricane force, that blow down out of these mountains during the fall and winter. The environmental benefit of these powerful winds is evident in their ability to scour the air—turning it a brilliant blue against the rocky gray mountains. Tucked into the base of this dramatic setting is the newest of the colleges of the Los Angeles Community College system, Los Angeles Mission College. After years of holding classes in storefront locations this community lobbied successfully for a new home. While many of the buildings for the new campus were designed and built, the cornerstone building, the library/learning resource center had been postponed until now. This facility symbolizes all of the aspirations of this community. It is where their youth will take their first steps toward finding a career and a passion. It is where the adult community can come to continue their exploration of knowledge and it is where the elders of the community can come to connect with the generations beyond their own while renewing their skills and fulfilling their vision.

The building design had to bridge literally and metaphorically. It had to open to the surrounding community and serve as the gateway to the campus, reaching out with large windows to embrace the view of the mountains to the north. Located on a steeply sloping site, it had to link the levels of the campus to make whole the fabric that had been initiated with the original campus design while sheltering the occupants from the powerful winds. It had to complete the open ended quad that was the primary gathering place on campus and it had to reach out to the virtual universe of technology that exists beyond the physical boundaries of the college walls. Built on three levels,

1

3   The distance learning lecture hall hosts a variety of lectures and classes, and is electronically linked to a state-wide community college and California State University distance learning system
4   The technology-level central circulation atrium introduces light and air and facilitates internal oversight
5   The campus quad entry lobby allows solar heat gain and expansive natural light without affecting computer workstations beyond

the program is zoned to provide optimal links between all of the elements: a print material library on the upper level with street access from the neighborhood; a learning resource center with 500 networked work stations on the middle level with direct access from the campus quad, and production space for TV and radio broadcasts and production on the lower level with direct access to a sunken courtyard filled with natural light. Bridging between the lower and middle levels is the distance learning lecture hall, which is fully networked and links with broadcast programming sent to other partner colleges and brings programming into the hall from the far reaches of the virtual environment.

4

5

Permanence and Transition

Permanence is an illusion. Or, ironically, the only permanence is transition. We build with the intent that our structures will last through the ages and yet we are surrounded by currents that erode that permanence and rush past on their way to the sea. We seek to preserve elements that offer clues about our past. We uncover the layers of indiscretion to restore all that we value to its radiant glow. Moving forward is the only direction and yet we long to remain stationary for a moment. To hold back the swirling current we transform our resources into places that capture time. Is it possible to create truly timeless design? It often seems that the more one tries to detach from time and place, the less successful the outcome is. The most timeless structures are at the same time the most indigenous. An old stone house constructed of native materials using the techniques of the time captures the essence of being timeless by not trying. Transition is continuous and never ending. We adapt, change in small increments, and modify to suit our current activities. We embrace transition by designing to not stand in its way. The layers of a building vary in their ability to accept change. Perhaps our most conscious effort to embrace transition is in creating a framework of great permanence that has the ability to survive the environment in which it stands and yet shelter within its walls and roof an ever-evolving pattern of life.

What is the signpost at this intersection? The answer is respect for age and recognition of the value of something that has existed for years. Why is it that a re-creation of a historic place never feels authentic? There is a patina that only time can yield. There is no rushing it; there is no faking it. Only time can apply that layer of meaning. This is why it is so critical to understand the impact of altering what time has created. When venturing into the forest to construct a house, one could clear the land and then replant trees to replace those removed. Given another 100 years the forest may return in an altered form, but it will not be the same place. Entering that same forest and building among the trees offers a far different outcome.

Beverly Vista Elementary School Historic Renovation and Addition

Design/Completion 2003/2007
Beverly Hills, California
Beverly Hills Unified School District
25,000 square feet

Building structure
Steel frame with concrete-reinforced brick masonry walls; single-story elements are wood framed with conventional concrete footings

Building materials
Restored brick exterior walls; salvaged clay roof tile; replicated wood windows with high-efficiency glazing, energy efficient HVAC and lighting systems; interior materials with high recycled content; water saving plumbing fixtures

Heavily damaged by the 1994 Northridge earthquake, Beverly Vista School, Building B stood as a monument to all that could succeed or fail on this historic campus. The last remaining structure from the original 1920s brick collegiate gothic campus, Building B housed the campus auditorium and the iconic bell tower that had been a landmark in the community, since its construction. Having withstood the Long Beach earthquake of the 1930s and steady redevelopment of the surrounding community, it was empty and boarded up for more than a decade, slowly succumbing to the ravages of bird and insect damage. The district and community were steadfast in their desire to preserve this cultural asset as a symbol of permanence in a rapidly changing environment and to give it new life as a vital asset for the students.

After significant review and planning, the district gave direction that the historic auditorium and adjacent tower should be preserved and renovated. This would be coupled with the construction of a new facility—to complement the historic theme of the structure while providing the required programmatic spaces in a contemporary facility. The program identified 11 new classrooms including a band room, choral music room, two language labs, and a reading room area. The façades facing Charleville Boulevard to the north and Rexford Drive to the east are the most visible to the surrounding community and have been developed in a manner sensitive to that neighborhood. The other existing structures on the Beverly Vista site, located to the south, are new and were constructed to replace the earthquake-damaged buildings of the original campus. The materials and many of the decorative elements of these new buildings were selected to echo the structures they replaced. The new façades of Building B and its reconstruction toward the south and facing South Elm Drive were similarly developed in a manner sensitive to the newly constructed structures of the campus and of the neighborhood.

1

1 The corner perspective illustrates the meeting of old and new
2 The bell tower anchors the residential corner and serves as the primary entrance to the theater
3 The tower lobby retains the original historic painted wood veiling, pendant-light fixture, and brick floor; the new doors have been custom-fabricated to match other existing restored doors

2

3

4 The floor plan reveals the extensive
addition made to the existing historic
building

5 A choral and rehearsal room is
inherently flexible to accommodate a
variety of activities

6 The restored historic theater retains
the original detailing and is graced by
the original wood stage and ceiling

7 The music room is acoustically tuned
to support a magnate program in the
performing arts

8 A typical classroom is zoned for quiet
and active learning options through
the use of reflective versus absorptive
surfaces, and lighting options

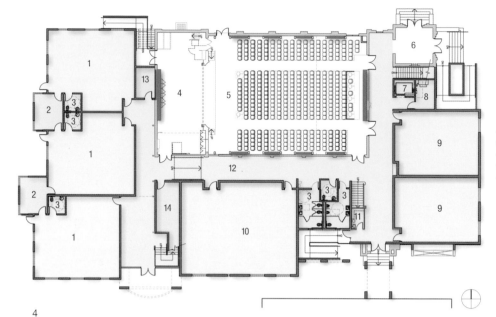

1 Kindergarten
2 Teaching preparation
3 Toilet
4 Stage
5 Auditorium – 380 seats
6 Tower
7 Elevator
8 Elevator equipment
9 Classroom
10 Choral room
11 Janitor closet
12 Corridor
13 Storage
14 Green room/storage room

4

5

6

7

8

The renovation of the historic structures was resource intensive. The roof was removed and the interior gutted to allow for the installation of new footings under the massive unreinforced brick walls. The walls were secured with a new gunite shell and a new steel roof was utilized to tie the entire structure together. Historic features were both preserved in place and removed and reinstalled in the renovated facility. Brick and roof tiles salvaged from the original facility were woven into the new buildings to tie them together into a cohesive fabric. Two massive trees were protected in place and form the heart of the newly landscaped courtyard that links the south and north elements of the campus.

The greatest reward for all followed the completion of the project as person after person from the community gathered in the restored auditorium and reflected on the days they had spent as students over the past 80 years within the walls of the Beverly Vista School. One dignitary stood at the podium on the stage, looked out at the standing-room-only crowd and said, "The last time I stood on this stage and looked out I was speaking to my fellow eighth grade classmates and running for Class President. I have those same butterflies today!"

Entomology Laboratory and Research Facility

Design/Completion 1990/1994

Riverside, California

University of California, Riverside

9000 square feet

Building structure
Structural steel frame with metal deck; concrete foundations with concrete masonry unit retaining walls

Building materials
Painted exterior plaster with standing-seam metal roof; high-performance glazing in steel frames; sealed concrete floors; high-efficiency lighting and mechanical systems

The University of California, Riverside, began as the Citrus Experiment Station at the turn of the 20th century. Grand Spanish Revival structures mixed with austere ranch buildings to form the core of the campus. Over time the fabric grew to include a diverse mix of stark 1950s modern and bungalow buildings. The site selected for the Entomology Laboratory is at the nexus between one of the classic arched-loggia colonial buildings and a four-story horizontally banded 1960s building of white concrete and glass. Drawing inspiration from these forms, the Entomology Laboratory borrows gables and strong geometric forms from the vocabulary of its neighbors. Color is used to evoke memories of the warm palette of terracotta and greens from the landscape and tiled roofs that border the site.

Located on a small sloping site on the edge of the UC Riverside campus, the Entomology Laboratory and Research Facility houses the extensive entomology specimen collection and provides sophisticated laboratory and support spaces for students, researchers, and faculty. The ground floor of the facility embraces the pre-eminent collection of insects in the world—row upon row of carefully preserved and archived creatures from those that can barely be seen by the unaided eye to specimens the size of your hand. The heart of the building grew from the serious business of caring for this collection, studying specimens and understanding their behavior. At the same time it was impossible to ignore the whimsy of a large "bug house" with an abstracted vocabulary that is playful and spirited. Abstracted classical forms intertwine with sweeping curves to announce the energy of the people who bring this facility to life.

The laboratories are designed to meet the specialized needs of entomologists with temperature-controlled, isolated holding and rearing rooms. Due to the high probability that major earthquakes will occur, the fragile research projects are housed in a seismically isolated room. This ensures that the instruments utilized by researchers will survive any potential seismic events—averting the possible loss of years of experimental data.

1

1   Simple forms reflect the colors and shapes of the older surrounding campus structures
2   The museum draws the visitor into a distinctive home for research and display

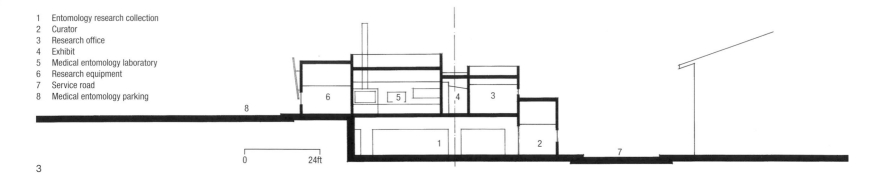

1 Entomology research collection
2 Curator
3 Research office
4 Exhibit
5 Medical entomology laboratory
6 Research equipment
7 Service road
8 Medical entomology parking

0   24ft

3

4

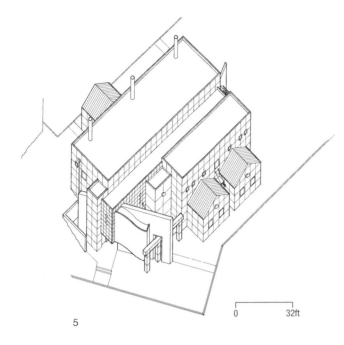

5

A rare collection of insects is housed in environmentally controlled museum space that serves the general university population for general education as well as the world-class scientific research staff. The success of this project is due to its highly functional and flexible plan, its keen awareness of the contextual site issues, its aesthetic balance and clarity, and its integration with the department's mission.

0   32ft

6

7

3   Section
4   The laboratories themselves support a comprehensive curriculum in entomology specific to California agricultural studies
5   Axonometric
6   The primary entrance to the building playfully represents the insects found within the museum exhibits
7   The building steps down a hillside adjacent to historic campus buildings

Anaheim Children's Station

Design/Completion 1991/1993

Anaheim, California

City of Anaheim

9500 square feet

Building structure
Original wood framed structure was
restored and placed on new concrete
foundations; addition is wood framed
to match historic structure

Building materials
Exterior painted plaster, metal trellises
with native plantings for shade and
ornament, high-performance glazing,
recycled content carpeting and tiles,
low-VOC finishes on the interior and
exterior; casework core material is
non-toxic and non-off-gassing

The railroad and its service to the growing city of
Anaheim during the 19th and early 20th centuries were
seen as signs of permanence and prosperity. As the last
century came to an end and transportation shifted to
other modes, the Anaheim train station was left as a
sentimental icon in town, but it fell on hard times. The
station was a victim of termite and dry rot damage, and
was saved only by the rescue efforts of local preservation
groups. In danger of physical collapse, the building was
"cut off at the knees," placed on jacks and held in a state
of arrested decay.

This building in search of a use seemed particularly ripe
for childlike activity. The need for childcare in this
renewed area of Anaheim was strong and it became
clear that bringing this community service together with
the desire to preserve a small slice of history would
benefit a broad cross section of the population. The
Anaheim Children's Station is a unique project,
supporting the adaptive reuse of this existing structure to
anchor the downtown redevelopment. The playful
combination of a historic building with a new addition
provides a positive environment receptive to parent
involvement through close proximity to home and work.
The project adds 5500 square feet of reception,
administration, meeting room, full kitchen, classrooms,
and support facilities for 77 infants, toddlers, and pre-
schoolers to the restored historic structure of the original
train station. Adjacent to a neighborhood park, the center
links to the outdoor space and offers the opportunity to
bring generations together in a common setting.

Getting the structure to its permanent home was a feat
in itself. The site is actually about two blocks from the
original railway station site. Due to redevelopment
pressures the building had to be relocated to make way
for the planned uses in the downtown. Cribbed up and
supported, the building as a whole unit was slowly
moved across the existing railway bridge on the old
tracks to the other side of town. There it was gently
placed on new foundations and restored to its current
splendor. The building has assumed its rightful place
as a focal point for all of the residents.

1 Nighttime restores the old train station to its former splendor as a
  community icon
2 The former station was moved over a railroad bridge and across
  the tracks to its new location within the civic center neighborhood
3 Play structures were specifically selected to reflect the features of
  the historic building
4 The design of the infant–toddler room illustrates the application of
  the colors of the old train station with the introduction of
  contemporary programmatic solutions

1

2

3

4

Chapman Hills
Elementary School

Design/Completion 1988/1991

Orange, California

Orange Unified School District

45,000 square feet

Building structure
Wood-framed structure with steel columns; lightweight steel truss roof; conventional concrete foundation

Building materials
Composition shingle roof to match adjacent residential construction, manufactured wood siding from recycled wood products, high-efficiency glazing, high-efficiency lighting HVAC with computerized energy management system and distributed controls; natural light and ventilation; high recycled content throughout project; classroom walls covered in fabric to accept Velcro

The Irvine Ranch valley chosen as the site for Chapman Hills Elementary School was, only a few years before, the center of a vast agricultural complex. Outbuildings for the ranch could still be found dotting an occasional field, but they were destined to fade, lost to future generations who might no longer understand the deep roots that existed in this place. This new school was being created at a time when most institutions were being housed in anonymous structures that evoked little excitement for any of the inhabitants. The challenge was how to design an environment that was cutting-edge in its approach to technology and the students' access to the expanding resource of the Internet, while evoking the memories that would anchor this building to its site and the dreams of the students. To borrow from an author of that time, John Naisbitt, we wanted to be "high tech and high touch."

There were practical issues to overcome as well. The client had just re-roofed 43 schools and did not want any flat-roofed buildings. The location is surrounded by residential sites on all four sides—all of which had views looking down into the school. The district also wanted to test an old concept that had become new again for California—to place the entire school under one roof with no exterior covered walkways and every space linked to create a sense of unity and shared resources among all of the students and teachers.

The resulting design grew from the iconic forms of farm buildings with their simple gabled roofs, clerestories, and vertical cylindrical forms. The profile also echoes the caricatures that children draw when asked to sketch a schoolhouse. The large sloping central roof reaches out to embrace the classrooms clustered around the perimeter, each cluster sharing a central technology space and allowing teachers to partner throughout the day. The central space is meant to provide images of a barn-like loft with its trussed roof and high natural light. This is the hub for all activities. It serves as multipurpose space, library, and head end for all campus technology. A joint-use agreement with the city gave access for the students to the adjacent parkland

1

1 An adjacent city park provides shared playfields, while the school site
provides a small silo building to house restrooms and segregated storage
2 The architectural style harkens back to the days of the one-room country
schoolhouse on what was formerly ranch property

3   The central library/media circulation desk shares open space with the library media center and multipurpose room; sustainable strategies are evident in the lighting and operable clerestories

4   Floor plan illustrates the organizational clusters toward a central core; the east elevation is typical of the agrarian style of the original farm buildings occupying the site

5   The kindergarten classrooms have high clerestories with operable windows, energy-efficient lighting with sensors, tackable/acoustical walls, and high-performance glazing

6   The adjacent city park provides joint-use opportunities for sports and recreational activities

1   Entry
2   Reception
3   Clerical
4   Resource
5   Resource desk
6   Computer/audio/video
7   Media center
8   Faculty lounge
9   Patio
10 Amphitheater
11 Classroom
12 Tech center
13 Kindergarten
14 Maintenance
15 Kitchen
16 Lunch shelter
17 P.E. storage
18 Computer/audio/video

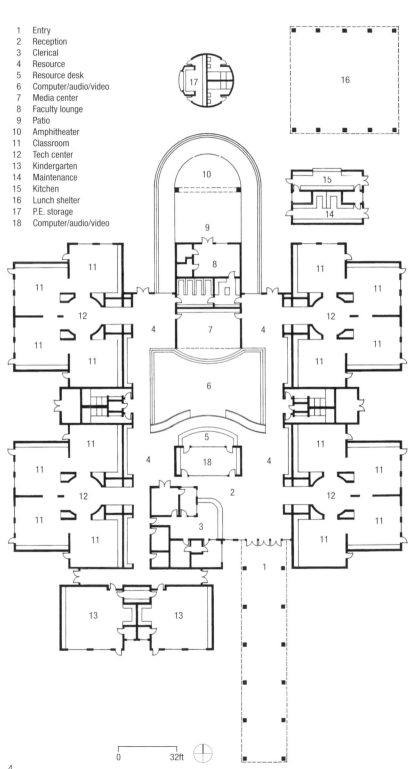

0   32ft

3

4

with its athletic fields. In exchange, the school provides a silo-like building housing toilet rooms and storage for athletic equipment. This allows utilization of the facility around the clock without compromising the security of the school's interior.

In the impermanence of Southern California this project serves to remind all who visit that there once was a ranch on this site—a history of the area using buildings in place of words. As we transition to the future with technology infusing every element of our lives, it is reassuring to have a place that gently links us with that past.

6

5

Awards

Dougherty + Dougherty Architects LLP is fortunate to have been distinguished with local, state, regional, and national design awards. Individual projects have been recognized for their unique response to their respective parameters.

2007 Concrete Masonry Association
  of California & Nevada
Sustainable Design – Merit Award
Crozier Middle School

2007 Concrete Masonry Association
  of California & Nevada
Education Design – Merit Award
Crozier Middle School

2007 National School Board Association
Exhibition of School Architecture
Crozier Middle School
Lucille Smith Elementary School

2005 UC/CSU Environmental Award –
  Best Sustainable Project
Fullerton Arboretum

2005 Gold Nugget Award of Merit
Mountain Residence, Mammoth Lakes

2005 National School Board Association
Exhibition of School Architecture Citation Winner
Lucille Smith Elementary School

2004 AIA Orange County Honor Award
Cameron Park Community Center and Gymnasium

2004 Concrete Masonry Association
  Award of Merit
Cameron Park Community Center and Gymnasium

2004 Gold Nugget Award of Merit
Cameron Park Community Center and Gymnasium

2003 American Institute of Architects
  Orange County Chapter Merit Award
Warren Lane Middle School

2002 American Association of School
  Administrators National Award
Rio Del Norte Elementary school

2002 AIA Orange County President's Award
Brian P. Dougherty, FAIA and Betsey Olenick
Dougherty, FAIA

2002 AIA Orange County Merit Award
Lucille Smith Elementary School

2002 Education Design Showcase Awards
Rio Del Norte Elementary School

2002 Education Design Showcase Awards
Diane Bollinger Memorial Gymnasium

2002 National School Boards Association
Rio Del Norte Elementary School

2002 National School Boards Association
Crozier Middle School

2002 CASH Design Awards
Westside Elementary School

2001 American School and University
Rio Del Norte Elementary School

2001 CASH Design Awards
Culver City High School Photo Lab

2000 Education Design Showcase Awards
California State University Dominguez Hills
    Extended Education Campus

2000 Education Design Showcase Awards
Thousand Oaks High School Performing Arts Center

2000 American School and University
California State University Dominguez Hills
    Extended Education Campus

1999 AIA Orange County, Environmentally
    Responsive Design Award
John Lyle Center for Regenerative Studies

1999 CASH Award of Merit
Ocean Park Elementary School

1998 American School and University
Ocean Park Elementary School

1998 AIA Orange County, Environmentally
    Responsive Design Award
Ocean Park Elementary School

1998 AIA Orange County, Merit Award Winner
Warehouse Studio

1998 Merit Award, Pacific Coast Builders
    Conference
Tustin Family and Youth Center

1998 California Parks & Recreation
    Society Award
Tustin Family and Youth Center

1998 Architecture and the Environment
John Lyle Center for Regenerative Studies

1997 Woodwork Institute of California
    Award for Excellence
L.A. Mission College Library/Learning
    Resource Center

1997 AIA California Council Nathaniel
    A. Owings Award
John Lyle Center for Regenerative Studies

1996 CASH Design Award
Garfield Elementary School

1995 AIA California Council Presidential Citation
ADAPT Program

1995 California Parks & Recreation Society
    Award of Excellence
Citrus Park Day Care Center

1994 U.S. Department of Energy Ten Best
    Environmental Projects
John Lyle Center for Regenerative Studies

1994 AIA California Council Distinguished
    Service Citation
Betsey Olenick Dougherty, FAIA

1994 President's Award, American Institute
    of Architects
Betsey Olenick Dougherty, FAIA

1994 SCE Grand Award
John Lyle Center for Regenerative Studies

1994 California Women in Environmental
    Design Citation of Excellence
John Lyle Center for Regenerative Studies

1994 CASH Design Award
Ocean Park Elementary School

1994 CASH Design Award
Walker Elementary School

1994 National School Boards Association
Chapman Hills Elementary School

1994 National School Boards Association
Garfield Elementary School

1992 California Masonry Design Award
Garfield Elementary School

1992 CASH Design Award
Chapman Hills Elementary School

1989 Grand Award Pacific Coast Builders
    Conference
Seitz Residence

1989 Merit Award Pacific Coast Builders
    Conference
Seitz Residence

1989 Presentation at Monterey Design
    Conference
Schools

1987 Illuminating Engineers Society Honor Award
Dougherty + Dougherty Studio

1986 Judges' Commendation AIA Orange County
POD, Inc.

1985 Merit Award AIA Orange County
Dougherty + Dougherty Studio

1984 Honorable Mention AIA Orange County
Karlstad Residence

1983 Merit Award AIA Orange County
Heller Residence

1982 Honorable Mention AIA Orange County
Thomas Residence

1981 Women In Design International
Betsey Olenick Dougherty

Publications

Projects have been recognized through books, periodicals, and newspaper articles. The Center for Regenerative Studies is one of only four U.S. projects profiled in *Architects and the Environment*, published in London, England.

2007 *Profiles in Architecture*
Concrete Masonry Association of
  California & Nevada
Crozier Middle School

2007 *American School and University*
  Architectural Portfolio
Fullerton Arboretum

2007 *American School and University*
  Architectural Portfolio
Crozier Middle School

2007 *Learning by Design*
Lucille Smith Elementary School

2006 *Learning by Design*
La Mirada High School Classroom Addition

2006 *School Planning & Management*
Project of Distinction Award
Sierra Vista Elementary School
  Classroom Addition

2005 *American School and University*
  Architectural Portfolio
Fullerton Arboretum
Lucille Smith Elementary School

2005 Orange County *HOME* Magazine
Mountain Residence, Mammoth Lakes

2004 *Profiles in Architecture*
Concrete Masonry Association of
  California and Nevada
Cameron Park Community Center and
  Gymnasium

2004 *New York Times* Article (June 4)
Mountain Residence, Mammoth Lakes

2002 *Architectural Record Online*

2002 *Learning by Design*
Culver City High School Photo Lab
  Classroom Addition

2002 *Learning by Design*
Rio Del Norte Elementary School

2000 *Learning by Design*
L.A. Mission College Library Learning
  Resource Center
Rio Del Norte Elementary School
Thousand Oaks High School Performing
  Arts Center

1998 *Architecture and the Environment*
  Bioclimatic Building Design
Author: David Lloyd Jones
John Lyle Center for Regenerative Studies

1996 *Architectural & Business Poland*
John Lyle Center for Regenerative Studies

1995 *Byggenkunst*, The Architecture
  Magazine of Norway
Cover Story on John Lyle Center for
Regenerative Studies

1995 *Architectural Record* Magazine
Garfield Elementary School

1995 *Solar Today* Magazine
John Lyle Center for Regenerative Studies

1995 *Green Architecture*
Author: Michael Crosby
John Lyle Center for Regenerative Studies

1995 *Progressive Architecture/PA Plans*
Citrus Park Day Care Center

1994 *Architecture* Magazine Feature
John Lyle Center for Regenerative Studies

1994 *Architecture* Magazine
Garfield Elementary School

1994 *Landscape Architecture* Magazine
John Lyle Center for Regenerative Studies

1994 *Learning by Design* Magazine
Garfield Elementary School

1991 *Progressive Architecture* Magazine
Schools

1989 *Professional Builder* Magazine
Seitz Residence

1988 *Professional Builder* Magazine
Karlstad Residence

1986 *Interiors* Magazine
Dougherty + Dougherty Studio

1986 *L.A. Times Home* Magazine
Dougherty + Dougherty

1985 *Architecture California*
Brian P. Dougherty

1985 *L.A. Times Home* Magazine
Feature Article
Heller Residence

Acknowledgments

We would like to acknowledge the 175 individuals who have been a part of Dougherty + Dougherty over the past 29 years. Their energy, creativity, collaboration, and insight have informed each of these projects and built the foundations of ideas that have continued to push us to find new paths on this journey.

Photographers

Milroy & McAleer
Cameron Park Community Center and Gymnasium
Fullerton Arboretum Visitor Center and Events Pavilion
Newport Coast Community Center
Anaheim Children's Station
Tustin Family and Youth Center
LA Mission College Library Learning Resource Center
John Lyle Center for Regenerative Studies
Thousand Oaks High School Performing Arts Center
Entomology Laboratory and Research Facility
California State University, Dominguez Hills – Extended
    Education Campus
Ocean Park Elementary School
Chapman Hills Elementary School
Garfield Elementary School
Rio Del Norte Elementary School
Walker Elementary School
Mountain Residence

Standard Photography
Crozier Middle School
Lucille Smith Elementary School

Ron Moore/ RMA Photography Inc.
Heller Residence

Orrin Moore/ RMA Photography Inc.
Beverly Vista Elementary School Historic Renovation
and Addition

Dougherty + Dougherty Architects LLP
Cameron Park Community Center and Gymnasium
Fullerton Arboretum Visitor Center and Events Pavilion
Newport Coast Community Center
Anaheim Children's Station
Tustin Family and Youth Center
Apple Valley Town Hall Expansion
John Lyle Center for Regenerative Studies
Entomology Laboratory and Research Facility
California State University, Dominguez Hills – Extended
    Education Campus
Education Operation Support Center
Culver City High School Photo Lab Addition
La Mirada High School Classroom Addition
Crozier Middle School
La Tijera K–8 School
Rio Del Norte Elementary School
Ocean Park Elementary School
Chapman Hills Elementary School
Mountain Residence